You Are A City

*Alchemists, Flaneurs, and
the Psychic Experience of Urbanism*

Will Selman

Copyright © 2025 by Will Selman
ISBN 979-8-218-88904-3

All rights reserved. No part of this publication may be reproduced or transmitted in any form or by any means, mechanical or electronic, including photocopying and recording, or by any information storage and retrieval system, without permission in writing from the author and/or publisher.

All permissions for quotes and images are held by the author, who releases the publisher from all liability.

Also by Will Selman
Temenos

symbolicurbanism.org
urbanevolutionary.wordpress.com

Cover art source unknown
Photographs by the author unless otherwise noted
Layout by Rachel Lambert, rlambertdesign.com

"No eternal reward will forgive us now for wasting the dawn."

—*Jim Morrison*

Table of Contents

Introduction 1

I. An Evolutionary Spirituality 5
- *The Story of Human Psychic Awakening*
- *A Short History of Mythology*
- *The Cycles of History*
- *The Democratization of Osiris*
- *The Great God Pan is Dead!*
- *The Bicameral Mind and the Ages of the Zodiac*
- *The Trend Toward Greater Complexity and Connection*
- *The City and Jungian Psychology*

II. The Meaning of the City 23
- *Why Cities Exist*
- *The First City-Builders*
- *Non-western Cities Built as Spiritual Metaphor*
- *Greek and Roman Ideals*
- *Medieval Europe*
- *Faust and His City*
- *The Contemporary American Experience*

III. Archetypal Elements of the City 37
- *What Are Archetypes?*
- *What They Are Not*
- *The Role of Symbols, Metaphor, and Myth*
- *Basic Jungian Archetypes*
- *Some Basic Archetypal Urban Elements*
- *Making Use of Urban Archetypes*

IV. The City as a Classroom:
Spiritual Development and Psychic Exploration 53
- *Incarnation on Earth: A Boarding School Experience*
- *A New Perspective on Nature*

- *A Stage for the Senses*
- *Cities and Storytelling*
- *Dreaming and Waking in the Streets of Paris*
- *Bridges: Infrastructure and Relationship*
- *Sewers and the Jungian Shadow*
- *Weather, Seasons, and the Time of Day*

V. **The Alchemists**...85
- *A Brief History of Alchemy*
- *Their (mostly) Unconscious Methods*
- *Jung and His Alchemical Psychology*
- *The Stages of Alchemical Psychic Transformation*
- *An Urban Alchemy for Today*

VI. **The Flaneur**..101
- *What a Flaneur Does*
- *Tai Chi and Meditative Walking*
- *How to Discover a New City*

VII. **The City as Meditative Labyrinth**...........................109
- *The Story of Labyrinths*
- *Labyrinth or Maze?*
- *City Streets as a Template*
- *Dupont Circle: An Example*

VIII. **A Process of Introspection**..................................117
- *On Ritual*
- *The Everyday*
- *Dreams*
- *Active Imagination: The Importance of Non-Existent Places*
- *Three Tasks of Life*
- *You Are A City: Urbanism as a Tool for Expanding Spiritual Horizons*

Afterword..143
Sources and Further Reading....................................146

You Are A City

Introduction

"I will arise now, and go about the city, through its streets and squares, and search for the One my heart loves."—Song of Songs 3:2

This is a book about connecting more deeply with soul by making use of the city as a tool and setting for psychic exploration. The city itself is here understood as the embodiment of collective soul, and its elements reflect the inner complexity of our individual souls. Physical urban space is rarely thought of in such a way; normally we assume that spiritual activities ought to take place in a quiet room or in green nature like a mountaintop or under a tree by a stream, or a wild beach at sunset. While that is of course appropriate, I say that the city also can provide such a setting. Beyond that, what this book seeks to promote is an understanding of civilization, including both cities and our individual inner lives, as a series of long cycles of human psychic development over tens of thousands of years. We are in the midst of in the midst of yet another dramatic shift in these ongoing cycles of history, and the city – or town, village, or neighborhood- is a highly valuable tool in our understanding of this process. It can provide insights into not only one's personal journey of inner growth, but also the ongoing project of human psychic evolution.

We are all on a spiritual path, looking for something, with only a vague idea of what that might be. Some may prefer thinking more along the lines of psychological growth rather anything religious or spiritual, but the need remains the same no matter the terminology we prefer, or even if we are unaware of it. But why think of the city in such a fashion? Is it not too loud, dirty, and, well, all too human? Why the city and not wild nature? Well, of course nature can provide an ideal setting; it has been our home since our beginnings. However, the human experience is becoming ever more urban. Population is expected to grow over the next 15 years (barring utter catastrophe) by one billion people. To keep up with that growth, we will need to build the equivalent of a new city of 1.5 million people every week. As a social species, we are becoming ever more urbanized; our daily experience is not of wild nature but of buildings and pavement. Our experience of the city must be redeemed.

The soul cares about the places we build and what we can experience. The soul wants to be a part of everything we create, and the city is our largest creation. The soul tells us to seek the eternal by delving more deeply into temporal - this particular time and this specific place.

The gods are gone and conventional religion is rapidly fading, but the psychological needs they once addressed and gave life to are still very much with us. Religion and mythology were once the tools we used to interact with our inner psychic life. We have discarded those tools but the work they performed is still necessary. As a result, we have decanted ourselves out of traditional church buildings as well as modes of thinking. We stand outside without the psychological protection they once provided. We now find ourselves out on the metaphorical city sidewalk. Can that urban experience fill a gap?

We find ourselves alienated; separated from society, nature, from one another, from our own self. We say society is psychotic or schizophrenic, unable to distinguish real from unreal. We have no goals or purpose individually or culturally, and no guideposts, no cultural memory in the form of myth and metaphor. We need to re-establish some guideposts, both personally and collectively; finding them in our everyday experience is an obvious way to start. Understanding the city as a collection of potential guides opens up so many doors to the inner life.

Cities are almost never designed, arranged, or intended for purposes of spiritual insight, at least not for several hundred years. I know of only one such place here in the United States. We can however create such a toolset for ourselves wherever we are.

The ancient world spoke of the city as a metaphor or symbol of the individual soul. Jesus is known to have said as much, that His followers will be the City of God, that we are the City of God. In the Coptic Bersianis codex, the son of god is called "the city with four gates." The psychologist Carl Jung, on whom we will lean heavily in the following pages, understood the city as representing the totality of the self – conscious and unconscious united – the indestructible city or Temenos, the sacred precinct where all the split-off parts of the self are brought together.

There are two fundamental assumptions driving this book. First is that the essential task of humanity, throughout all of time and cultures, is that of spiritual quest. This has both a personal and collective aspect, and is evolutionary in nature. That is, over the centuries humanity awakens to greater and larger insight. The second assumption is that the built environment has a basic role to play in that process, that the shape and design of our cities and towns can and should support this quest. As spirits embodied in the physical realm we are blessed with the opportunity to discover the eternal through our experience of the temporal.

Most of us imagine that the intention of a spiritual life is to connect with God, or whatever term we choose as a substitute – The First Cause, the Ultimate Ground of Being, Source, Energy, and so on. But to do so requires a couple of preliminary steps. First is the encounter with the personal soul, including the dark shadow, which is in itself difficult enough. Then the encounter with the collective soul/ unconscious. Together these two provide us with the "god image" – what we might call the mask of god, which that ultimate creative force of many names must wear in order for us to communicate. The city itself can be thought of as one of these masks. Only after wrestling with all of this can we even consider any real interaction with the Eternal. And that interaction consists mainly of silence and stillness. The city, precisely because it is rarely silent or still, is an unexpected resource and thus an enormous support in those preliminaries. A wonderful poem by the Sufi mystic, Rumi, tells us, "There is a community of the spirit; join it, and feel the delight of walking in the noisy street, and be the noise." To know God then, is to know oneself. We can seek the eternal, and find our inner self, by delving more deeply into this particular time and this particular place.

The following pages will cover a variety of ideas and methods to assist in this. Before diving in, some context and background are needed. This will cover some thoughts on who we are, what it means to be human, and how cities have played a role in the past as a setting for spiritual quest. Then we will look at various techniques, of both personal psychic examination and of urban exploration. These will include aspects of experiencing the city as path – "flaneury," alchemy, walking meditation, the labyrinth, and everyday activities such as drawing, writing, adopting, participating. Finally, each chapter will conclude with a set of questions to ponder.

There are innumerable methods and techniques to assist the unconscious in speaking with us and revealing information. These methods of personal divination make use of such varied tools as tarot, astrology, I ching, tea leaves, palmistry, the casting of sticks and bones, and so forth. I would like to propose the addition of one more method to this toolkit; the psychic experience of the city. This is a process of observation and reflection, of both the inner and outer worlds, to discover how they parallel one another. The most significant lessons of life are only learned through experience. In my experiences of big cities and small towns, of their buildings, streets and blocks, people and activities, I find reflections of the inner life of my soul, turned inside out and manifested in the world. Let's begin to explore it all.

CHAPTER I

An Evolutionary Spirituality

---

*"I have much more to say to you,
but you are not ready to hear"—John 16: 12*

The Ancient of Days; by William Blake

WHY START A BOOK FOCUSED ON THE PSYCHIC experience of the city with an overview of such an obscure concept as the evolution of human consciousness? Context is so important. Our personal journey of self-development is never conducted in isolation. In order to develop and grow we need to have a deeper understanding of who we are – what we are – and how we came to this point in life. Gaining some knowledge of how our ancestors developed gives us a better understanding of what we face now, both personally and collectively. Just as important, we need to remember that the places we build and how we experience them, reflect the values we hold. The fundamental sources of our values, in turn, are to be found in our deepest history, even preceding conscious awareness. So, in order to deepen and enrich our experience of our cities and towns – and ourselves – we must gain some understanding of our beginnings, and the various stopping points along the path we have travelled in the centuries since then. Below is a very cursory but hopefully sufficient overview of my thoughts on this.

The Story of Human Psychic Awakening

As a distinct species, we seem to have emerged quite recently, about 200,000 to 250,000 years ago. At roughly that point in time, archeologists find skeletal remains identical to ours today. We carry along with us into this new adventure a heritage of millions of years of instinctual habits and traits, which remain so deeply ingrained into us that we barely even think of them. Indeed, we don't even have a need to think of them; human instincts remain with us buried into our unconscious, cropping up constantly without our awareness. Have a fear of snakes? It's a holdover from our days as apes living in trees, when stepping on a poisonous snake was an everyday danger. Ever wonder where the idea of a dragon comes from? It represents a combination of two fears built into us as a safety device from our days as apes living in the trees of a jungle. Those snakes, living on the ground below us could bite and kill us, its venom burning like fire; a winged eagle or hawk, living above us, might swoop down from above and carry our children off for dinner. Combine these two common dangers of our ancient ancestors into one imaginal creature and you have a dragon, a fire-breathing snake with wings. These are no longer daily concerns but the reflexive instinct remains within us, developed into a mythological representation of danger.

Much of our lives today continue to be organized by such deeply ingrained fears and protective responses, without any conscious awareness on our part. We share this with our animal brethren. Yet gradually over the course of time, we developed something new, which has made us distinct from other species; a dramatically higher level of conscious self-awareness and memory. Roughly 150,000 years ago, evidence appears which shows humans beginning to make use of creative and artistic skills such as the use of decorative beads. Then a significant leap forward took place, according to archeologists such as Genevieve von Petzinger; about 50,000 years ago, signs appear of rituals, burial of the dead, and complex artistry. This is the point at which we humans truly began to act in ways that have no immediate survival benefit, but which reflect meaningful concerns for life after death, symbolism and artistry, and care for others; the beginnings of spiritual and moral life.

Prior to that point, we functioned purely out of our animal instinct. But then we started asking questions. We became aware of the future, its dangers and opportunities, and our mortality. My sense is that creation stories, which are universal in all ancient cultures but for us particularly found in that of Adam and Eve, are the mythologized memories of that transition into conscious awareness, which continues today. And again, from the Book of Genesis: "And God said: *'Let there be light!'*" which is a memory of that point in our development when we began to see, the point at which consciousness began to separate from unconsciousness. This provided us with the ability to imagine that which does not exist in the physical world. This is our great burden; possessing such an ability allows us to discover universal truths but also to lie. Such is the knowledge of good and evil. How should we respond?

Imagine the way in which we wake up in the morning. Slowly, we come to a vague groggy wakefulness, stretch and roll over, maybe blink and open one eye. Maybe we're not even really interested in waking up! We haven't had coffee or a shower yet. We look around trying to figure out what the day holds for us. It can be a painfully slow process. Now imagine an entire species going through that process of "waking up." It has taken tens of thousands of years for us as a species to awaken to even this low level of consciousness. We clearly are not yet fully awake.

Yet in the midst of that groggy, foggy, not-yet really-awake mind, we as a species began to do more than ask questions, but to seek and develop answers. We began this by telling ourselves stories.

A Short History of Mythology

Such is the story of our evolution - over millions of years biologically, hundreds of thousands of years psychologically, thousands of years culturally. We have been awakening from our deepest roots of pure unconscious animal instinct into self- directed conscious awareness. The role of religion and mythology, at their best, has always been to bear witness to that fumbling effort; to observe and try to make sense of this process of awakening. It is described in the story of Adam and Eve eating the apple in the Garden of Eden, the Greek myth of Prometheus stealing fire from the gods, and so on. "I exist?! Who and what am I? What is this place, where am I?" And most importantly, "how do I respond to my environment and how should I act around other people?" "What the hell is going on?!" Taken seriously, these are the most fundamental, and pretty frightening questions but we must face them.

The way humans have always confronted these is through a set of tools that fall under the headings of mythology and religion. Myth is important enough to humans that the psychologist Carl Jung felt that there is a fundamental myth-making instinct within the human species. Joseph Campbell has said, in his preface to *The Portable Jung*, that if the whole of civilization were to be wiped out in an instant, the very next generation would begin the entire effort at religious myth-making all over again.

Myth is not a description of a fictional event that took place once, long ago. Rather, it describes large, universal psychological occurrences that continue to happen, over and over, everywhere, all the time. The arrogance of Icarus, flying too close to the sun, is repeated today. King Arthur's Knights of the Round Table, setting off alone into the dark forest in search of the Holy Grail, is repeated today. And on and on. A myth can be understood as true, not because is historically factual or scientifically accurate, but because it is effective psychologically. Thus, myth is a form of therapy.

For most of our history, myth was an oral tradition of storytelling. There was no written tradition made up of books in a library. However, one way which myths were passed on through generations was through the starry constellations of the night sky. Constellations generally are named after characters from mythological stories. All cultures have such a tradition. Our ancestors thought of the stars at night as a library, where stories and tales are stored for recall at any time. Can we can think of the built environment of the city in the same way, functioning as a storehouse of mythic images? Rarely is a city designed with that sort of pedagogical intention. There are a few examples however, which we will explore in later chapters.

The great student and teacher of myth and religion, Karen Armstrong, describes a progression of stories and changing elaborations of myth and religion over time, to meet changing situations and insights. As I understand it, the flow is as follows:

- As a primate species, we acted out of simple instinct. This includes social systems and structures which we inherited from our simian ancestors. We created such social arrangements because they worked well enough to make life easier.

- Perhaps at some point after our earliest conscious awakening, we began to wonder, and ask questions. Why do we act this way?

- In order to reinforce a set of common social systems, we began to act out various cultural norms; the beginnings of ritual were intended to reinforce whatever habits were considered a social good.

- Myths began to develop as a way of explaining such rituals. The "great gods" and "giants" of ancient myth often represent long-forgotten individuals, or a group of such individuals, who first made some discovery or performed some great deed.

- The formation of myths and the enactment of rituals reinforced one another. Eventually, what we now understand as religion grew out of increasingly elaborate myth-making and formalized rituals.

The development of human myth has taken a number of shifts and leaps over the ages, according to Armstrong. There is a progression of stories and myths, along with the accompanying rituals and religions, which humans have developed as new situations arose and cultural realities shifted, requiring a new vision. It seems our earliest myths revolved around the Mother Goddess, and the animals we hunted and relied upon for survival. Then some 10,000 years ago we developed agriculture. This gave us a completely different way of understanding and relating to life. The sowing of seed, its nurture and harvest, provoked a new set of gods and stories. The creation and refinement of civilization into urban living, soon after the development of agriculture, required yet another completely different set of cosmological stories to help understand and order such a new way of living. This is the point at which a more rational way of living truly developed, accompanied by the rise of masculine gods usurping the place of the older Mother Goddess. What is termed the Axial Age, from roughly 800 to 200 BC according to Armstrong, then developed our mythical visions yet further. This involved integrating personal morality and cultural ethical ways of being, personal inner reflection, bringing a deeper relationship to the eternal than ritual and myth provided before. Teachers such as Lao Tzu, Buddha, the Greek philosophers, the Jewish prophets, and later, Christ, comprised this era. We are still reliant on the masters of this time to help determine our personal morality and collective ethical standards. Since then, starting about the year 1500 and particularly in the past 200 years, we in the West have become increasingly uncertain about the value of myth and religion. We can say, as does Armstrong, that we now live in a manner unprecedented in all of human experience. That is, we live without any guiding mythology. In large part this is due to the astonishing technology and economy that we now take for granted, which has created such a secure and stable society that we no longer worry about the inherent dangers of life. We no longer feel the need to look to myth for understanding; science, technology and financial models work so well, while myth is seen not only as useless but actually false. We no longer even have a sense of its original purpose. Wrestling with the psychic alienation produced by this overdevelopment of *logos* to the detriment of *psyche* is now our fate.

Hence the deep need for a practice of personal psychological and spiritual development. The remaining majority of this book will explore several methods we can undertake, in the midst of the physical world we have created for ourselves.

We have seen that myths are clearly not simple stories for entertainment. There are four functions of a mythology, according to Joseph Campbell, a leading scholar in the fields of mythology and comparative religion. These four basic functions are the mystical, cosmological, sociological, and pedagogical.

1. The **mystical** function is to awaken us to the mystery and wonder of creation, to open our minds and senses to an awareness of the mystical "ground of being," the source of all phenomenon;

2. The **cosmological** function is to describe the "shape" of the Universe and our world, so that it becomes vivid and alive to us, infused with meaning and significance. Every piece of creation has meaning and a role to play;

3. The **sociological** function is to pass down "the Law," the moral and ethical codes for people in a culture to follow, in order to define and support the prevailing social structure;

4. The **pedagogical** function is to lead us through particular rites of passage that define the significant stages of life, from childhood dependency to maturity to old age to death. These rites bring us into harmony with creation and allow us to make the journey from one stage of life to another, with a sense of security and purpose.

A myth will not reveal its lesson however, nor be truly understood, unless put into practice. This is done in two ways; a ritual powerful enough to transform one's life, and ethical action. These both emphasize experience over belief.

The Cycles of History

Considering history from a psychological perspective, not simply through a political or economic lens, is of enormous value and digs much deeper into human motivations. Jung's psychology of personal psychic development, or what he termed individuation, also has a cultural aspect. He saw that not only do individuals evolve psychologically over a lifetime, but so do civilizations, over the course of centuries.

We can think of our life here on earth as a school to which we are sent for a time. There is a well- known saying attributed to the Australian Aborigines: *"We are all visitors to this time, this place. We are just passing through. Our purpose here is to observe, to learn, to grow, to love…and then we return home."* As the years go on and centuries turn into ages, the lessons grow in complexity, building on what came before. Kindergarten is over whether we like it or not. The school calendar of life is moving on. Elementary school is over, time for high school, even if we aren't ready and haven't incorporated all the lessons. To try remaining in the past is like sticking with a kindergartner's Early Reader text into the college years.

As individuals we attend school for twelve years, sometimes more. For our human species, the academic years last much longer. It seems to me that religions and other systems of cosmological order retain their power to teach and inspire no more than roughly 2,000 years. Beyond that, human knowledge, experience, and values shift enough so that the old ordering system is no longer large enough to contain all the new insights, information, and experience. We living at a point in history when one of those 2,000-year cycles is ending; and as Jung phrased it, once the gods leave the temple, they never return.

The last 2,000 years have seen far more change and development than any other similar period, in the relatively short history of the human species of approximately 250,000 years. The last 200, and certainly the last 50 years, have seen a mind-numbing pace of change. Perhaps it has been too much for the majority of people to manage and incorporate into their private psychic lives, since we no longer even have a shared vision to ground us. The world is changing too fast for us to manage psychologically. Just stop the world already, dammit, I want to get off! Perhaps this is a basic source of our cultural and political discontent.

Civilization apparently cannot function well psychologically without some shared image of the Eternal; some final moral authority residing above humanity in some eternal realm beyond the political and cultural order of the day, that directs our vision of life and clarifies our moral decisions. Think in whatever term or image you like; God, Source, Energy, the Eternal. If we do not find some visionary compass in a religious system or spiritual practice, we will look for it elsewhere, and political movements will happily fill that void given the chance. For two thousand years that image has been provided to us in the West by the Christian tradition, flawed though we may see it now. But its authority and vision have faded to the point that today its evangelical followers rally around a particular set of political values in hopes of hanging on to its vision. The Christian era is out of gas so to speak; it is running on fumes with no substantial moral authority left at a cultural level. Yet to reject it without a sufficient replacement leaves us floundering. Something at least as psychologically powerful needs to replace it. But that is not anything we can ever invent; such visions of a unifying spiritual cosmological order arise from our collective unconscious, of their own accord. We can only wait, and prepare our own inner lives. This is a repeating cycle in history, as we shall see.

The Democratization of Osiris

I have alluded to the ongoing ages of history as stepping stones in the psychological development of humanity, or at least for the western heritage. Given our current state of affairs, it is an awfully difficult to accept that we are making much progress. Each generation seems to need slip back and must relearn the same old lessons, before moving forward. We can reach further back in time for examples, but let's focus on ancient Egypt to see how this can play out.

The Egyptian world was deeply occupied by the afterlife, which shaped its religion and politics. Pharoah was understood as the human incarnation of the god Horus, the only child of Osiris, who was the god of death and the giver of life. (see any comparison here with the Christian story?) As such, Pharoah's burial was a highly complex affair as preparation for life after death. Over time, his family desired this glory and privilege and was granted similar elevated status, mythologically, in the afterlife. The whole of the Egyptian aristocracy, being susceptible to jealousy just like the rest of us, felt that they too contained the same divine spark and desired a relationship to Osiris, and demanded and got the same cultural status for a glorious afterlife.

During their captivity in Egypt, the Israelites learned this story then expanded on it; *all* members of the tribal nation, not just an aristocracy, have access to salvation, all are imbued with a spark of the holy. Centuries later, Jesus expanded on this even further, saying not only members of the tribe, but *every* human is worthy and infused with that same divine spark.

There is an evolution here; the community of those considered worthy and suffused with the essential divine spark is to be increased and become ever more inclusive. And this evolutionary expansion continues; it is not over.

The Great God Pan is Dead!

The Roman author Plutarch tells us the story of Thamus, an Egyptian who was sailing from Greece to Rome. While near the Isle of Paxi, he and all his shipmates heard a loud voice call out, "Thamus, tell the world that the great god

Pan is dead." In the pantheon of the gods in the late classical world, Pan was on center stage as an essential figure. For the god Pan to be declared dead was a momentous and traumatic cultural shift. The story spread all around the Roman world, reaching even the Emperor Tiberius who asked to speak with Thamus. This occurred at a time when the world of Classical Rome and Greece was tiring of its gods and their accompanying mythic stories, filled with jealousy, rivalry, and petty bickering. The old stories, the cosmological vision that bound together the classical world, held less and less power for people. Please note this; that Tiberius reigned during the birth, life, and death of Jesus. The old gods were dying, and a new one had been born. These sorts of transitions take time however; not for another three hundred years did the Roman Emperor Constantine convert and truly begin the Christian age. We find ourselves in the same sort of "in-between times" today.

> *"God is dead. God remains dead. And we have killed him. How shall we comfort ourselves, the murderers of all murderers? What was holiest and mightiest of all that the world has yet owned has bled to death under our knives: who will wipe this blood off us?"—Nietzsche*

Friedrich Nietzsche wrote these words in his book The Gay Science, in 1887. What he was announcing was the death of the Christian faith. His words are much like the announcement that Pan was dead; Nietzsche is our version of Thamus, almost 2,000 years later. Another god has died; who is there to replace the old? There is no way to anticipate what the next cosmology might be, but it is safe to say that it will be as wildly different and unexpected as Jesus was in His day. And yet it will include and expand upon what has come before, just as always. The gods always die in this way, but they always resurrect too, in some new and unexpected form. There is no way to tell in what form, but there may be hints.

The Bicameral Mind and the Ages of the Zodiac

Yes, I am aware I am about to take a huge risk and raise a lot of hackles with the following, but let's give this a try, shall we? What we see in the political battles of today can be understood, in part, as a last gasp effort on the part of the "patriarchy" to hang on a little bit longer. But what we can hope for is not a return to "matriarchy," but a wedding of the two. Let me define these two terms, for I use them in a much different way than is common. By "patriarchy" I do not mean some sort of oppressive rule by men (although it often devolves into that), but the very idea of rationality. Science, quantitative analysis, bureaucratic procedure, hierarchy, technocracy, spreadsheets, engineering, a reductionist material view of the world. This approach to life began to develop perhaps 10,000 years ago with the rise of cities, civilization itself, and has provided huge benefits that none of us would ever relinquish. Prior to that, for who knows how many thousands of years, we seem to have operated in a much more "matriarchal" world of goddess worship. Today we can understand the "matriarchy" as an intuitive, nurturing, soulful approach to life and problem-solving. We find its expression in poetry, art, music, caretaking, metaphor, and so forth. Each gender of course has both within; women can take on a patriarchal attitude and men can operate with intuition. In this view, "patriarchy" and "matriarchy" can both nurture and oppress. But since the Enlightenment and the scientific revolution, for about the past 400 years, we have so overemphasized rationality in our civilization that the collective psyche has become wildly unbalanced. This is a fundamental source of our cultural neurosis. The writer and neuroscientist Iain McGilchrist describes this as a neurological battle within the "bicameral mind." The two halves of the human brain operate in different ways; one more rational and discriminating, the other more intuitive and global in its perspective. A new sense of the two, equally valued as partners, is called for.

Here is another wildly unconventional way of thinking about history that I find very useful as an organizing principle. That is, these grand shifts in the ages of history coincide, in some approximate fashion, to the ages of the zodiac. It seems that the grand overarching cosmological visions, myths, and religions that organize a civilization last more or less up to 2,000 years. After that, their energy dissipates- their vision no longer inspires because of various changes in a society. The vision is no longer large enough to accommodate all the new cultural advances in a society. Jung described the manner in which religious symbolism changes as being roughly parallel the ages of the zodiac, although to be clear, there is no direct causal relationship. Each of these ages seems to parallel, again very approximately, to stages of transition in religious metaphor. Taurus for instance, represented in the zodiac as a bull, reigned in the sky during a time when a bull was the standard sacrificial animal to the gods of the Middle East. Later, Moses warned his people to reject this ritual and take on the practice of sacrificing a ram or lamb; this coincided roughly with the beginning of the age of Aries, the ram. Jesus, centuries later, declared that He was the last sacrificial lamb and that His followers would be "fishers of men," all of which took place at the beginning of the age of Pisces, the astrological sign of the fishes. Today after not quite 2,000 years, Aquarius, the Water-bearer is beginning a new period of history.

The hippies of the 1960's were correct in announcing the coming age of Aquarius; their mistake was in thinking it would be a time of "love and light, positive vibes only." Yet awfully difficult times must be faced first, as one age and its values dies and another begins. As a sign of the zodiac, Aquarius is signified as a man carrying and pouring a jug of water. Water is a universal mythological symbol of the depths of the unconscious or the soul, and thus functions as a metaphorical call to inner reflection. At precisely the same time, another "water bearer" confronts us; climate-induced sea-level rise. Is the concept of sustainability enough to function as a decent response? What is it we are trying to sustain? A set of unsustainable habits and assumptions. But water is telling us something else. We are about to get swamped, literally and psychologically, by deep waters.

The Trend Toward Greater Complexity and Connection

There seems to be no discernable, specific end goal that evolution aims toward. The goal of biological evolution seems to be much more practical, of finding the most appropriate, efficient, and sustainable set of forms and patterns given an ever-changing environment. With this caveat; the trend that the evolutionary process does seem to emphasize over time is that of ever-increasing complexity and inter-connection. In his highly provocative book, Nonzero, Robert Wright outlines this evolutionary preference and its impact not only regarding biological systems, but also those of astrophysics, culture, and political organization as well. To my mind then, we can think of evolution as an organizing system that does not simply move us from bacteria to ape to human, but from simplicity and isolation to complexity and connection. My own observations tell me that a psychological goal for a human life in this movement toward connected complexity is the fundamentally human desire and need for meaning.

This search for meaning is of course a psychological process. Our growth, psychologically or spiritually, involves continually exploring and integrating new insight and knowledge. This is painful because it requires us to let go of once cherished and reliable assumptions that have become outmoded. Merely becoming a master of maintaining a set of boundaries is inadequate; we must also continually expand our boundaries. One must step outside of the known to accomplish this. Using the conventional western image of this, Christ is the representation of one who willingly accepts this process of death and renewal.

With this perspective of psychological evolution, we can consider that the original sin of the Old Testament was to have become conscious. This is found in the story of the Garden of Eden, in which we were free of conscious acts and functioned purely on animal instinct. We were cast out of the easy completeness of unconscious instinct when we awoke into consciousness and thus began also acting out of intention. Yet here we are, bearing an unbearable responsibility. Worse, the follow-up sin of today is to remain only half awake. In our normal semi-conscious state of everyday living, we remain subject to our old animal instinct but with little to no understanding, let alone control over ourselves.

All in or not at all; once awakened as a species, there is no going back for any of us. Vanishingly few of us are "all in," able to rise to the challenge. This is I suspect the admonishment in the Book of Revelations against remaining "lukewarm," neither awake nor asleep.

In trying to understand the process of evolution and its psycho-spiritual implications, I was struck by the idea of selective breeding. We have been breeding various plants and animals for millennia; the development of civilization itself is a sort of intentional breeding is it not? Can we think of breeding as a sort of "intentional evolution?" This idea is not new but remains a bit controversial. Certainly, a process of self-improvement that we might choose to undertake is a sort of evolution of the self. We are seeking to reach a higher level of selfhood in some fashion… to "breed" a better self. Perhaps in the ancient days beyond prehistory, when humans first became conscious and self-aware as represented in the story of Adam and Eve, we moved ourselves beyond the natural unconscious process of evolution into one of conscious "intentional breeding," constantly seeking and striving. Part of this of course has to do with the settings in which we place ourselves. The original setting, according to the Old Testament, was known as Paradise. My understanding of the translation of the term "paradise" means "a walled garden." The natural environment for humanity is thus a place of harmonious balance of the natural and the urban. We need to "breed" more balanced and harmonious cities and towns in which we can consciously, intentionally evolve, individually and collectively, toward wholeness.

The City and Jungian Psychology

Religion, as a formal and ritualized elaboration of myth, fulfills a basic fundamental psychological need. It is even so basic as to act like an instinct for us. None of this is static of course; myth and creed develop over time to fit changing cultural norms and psychological needs and insights. But both Thamus and Nietzsche have told us that the god of their time, of their world and ours, had died. What comes next, for us, our children, and their descendants?

The contemporary understanding that we are "free" from oppressive religion is no great relief; the psychological need that religion responded to is still very much alive. For some few individuals, a more "secular" spirituality in the form of Jungian psychology could lead the way. Jung himself said his work was addressed not to those possessing religious faith, but those who no longer have any vision to rely upon. Indeed, Sonu Shamdasani, the editor of Jung's Red Book, has pointed out that Jung's work comprises a "religion in the making." A bold statement, but if we in the secular west can no longer reach God in any traditional sense, we can reach our souls – the unconscious, in Jung's modern parlance, in which any image of god lies.

With all this background, we must now ask, what of the city? How does this great physical artifact of creative human civilization, plug into these issues of psychic growth and spiritual connection? Several chapters will later examine this question. The exploration and experience of the city is a method of reaching out to our souls. As Jung made clear, there is no coming to full psychic health without relationship to place. This is the point at which we can begin ask what the role of the city can be for us. We can see that, just as our conscious psychic life and our myths have developed and expanded over the millennia, so has the meaning of our urban settings. The role a city can play in our lives has not nearly reached its potential, and must continue to develop. To develop a vision of that potential, it is necessary to first gain a sense of how our ancestors viewed their cities.

Questions to Ponder

- How has my own understanding of spiritual life developed over time?

- How might the sorts of places I expose myself to affect my psychological development?

- How has the belief system I value changed and developed over time?

CHAPTER II

The Meaning of the City

"The least of things with a meaning is worth more in life than the greatest of things without it."—Carl Jung

Mont St. Michel, France

23

YOU ARE A CITY

THE CITY IS BY NATURE AN ECONOMIC AND intensely political creation, yet we are looking for something so much deeper than politics. As Jung stated, "99% of politics is mere symptoms." And so, to understand the city and what it offers us, we must look much more deeply, to the psychology of myth and metaphor which surrounds the very idea of a city. As the professor of Classics Eva Brann once said, "The question of connecting justice to happiness is answered by bringing to light the soul in mythical shape… so the soul itself, its formal "constitution," is discovered by the raising and taking down of cities." There is always value in looking to the past for insight. In our search for finding a personal, soulful meaning in our experience of the city, we are well served to look at how our ancestors found meaning in their towns and cities, even if only in the very cursory manner I provide here.

Why Cities Exist

We can think of a building as externalized clothing. That is, it operates as a barrier to protect us from some of the physical and psychological dangers of the world. By extension, a city too is a form of "externalized clothing," providing a layer of protection. But clothing has become more than merely practical but offers us a way to display ourselves and our values, just as our buildings and cities have. Some are more gracious than others.

Most writing on the origins of urban living concentrate on commerce, increased efficiency, and protection from outside invaders. For instance, Malcolm Gladwell, a popular writer known for his ability to find unexpected connections and trends, has shown how cities succeed because of their ability to create wealth and reflect fundamental patterns of nature. For the author Geoffrey West, a particle physicist writing about the field of biology, cities exist for their efficiency.

His book, Scale, describes his discoveries regarding the way biological organisms, cities, and corporations grow, live, and die. He relates how the various biological systems that make up a body all scale, up or down, so that in a sense, a shrew is simply a scale model of an elephant. The essential finding is what might be called the "rule of 15%," applicable to both biological systems and urbanism. West has found that with every doubling in population size, a city sees a decrease of about 15% in the cost of infrastructure, and a simultaneous equivalent 15% increase in various socioeconomic benefits.

In a very real but counter-intuitive sense then, living in a city is a way of living in harmony with natural principles. Doesn't always feel like it though, does it? But harmony with nature involves more than simply being surrounded by greenery; it includes patterns and systems as well. A natural pattern for humans, beyond those of practical, financial, and commercial concerns, is that of storytelling. A foundation of storytelling is to imagine things which do not exist in the physical world. This is our distinctive human ability; with it, we can act not only out of instinct but with intention. This imagination can be used to either lie or to discover and communicate transcendent metaphorical truths. The latter is one of the softer, less "technical" purposes of a city.

The iconic writer on urbanism, Louis Mumford, recognized this, bringing together the practical and symbolic, telling us "The chief function of a city is to convert power into form, energy into culture, dead matter into the living symbols of art, biological reproduction into social creativity." For an even more succinct perspective than Mumford's, we can turn to Shakespeare to discover why cities exist; in his simple line he reminds us, "all the world's a stage." Cities provide us the best settings to tell our stories. There are all sorts of venues a city normally provides us for storytelling, whether we are on the stage or in the audience. Concert halls, libraries, opera houses, lecture halls, college auditoriums, art museums, church sanctuaries, the humble coffee shop. A classic stage for storytelling though, is one not thought of as such; the sidewalk and street corner. This informal setting is the most common stage on which we find ourselves, chatting with friends while walking or during chance encounters with acquaintances or random strangers. Some sidewalk locations are so well situated for finding an audience that chance encounters become semi-formalized. Centuries ago, London instituted a specific spot for the telling of stories, known as Speakers Corner. Since the 1700's, anyone has had the right to set up a soapbox and speak their mind to whatever audience cares to stop and listen. An urban setting then, whether grand metropolis or small town, provides us with all the excellent settings for hearing and telling our personal stories.

But a city does more than provide us with a larger audience to hear our story; a city also has a story to tell us. Ancient cities were often laid out as the physical reflection of some cosmological or spiritual order; an attempt to recreate heaven on earth. Dozens of cities in ancient cultures—Mayan, Aztec, Chinese, Egyptian, Indian—show patterns reflective of cosmological or cultural belief systems. Like participating in an elaborate religious ceremony, residents might have had the daily sense of being immersed in, and participating in, a grand mythological story. Perhaps surprisingly, even Washington DC was designed with such a pattern in mind. Simply being in a significant place, walking down the street, can provide the opportunity to participate as an actor in a story or play. The ancient Andean city of Tiahuanaco in Bolivia built well over 1,000 years ago, seems to have been designed expressly for this purpose. As well as serving as the seat of a pre-Incan empire, it seems to have acted largely as a tourist attraction, as an expression of the empire's cosmic significance. Some archeological researchers speculate that the builders seemed to have intentionally kept the place unfinished, constantly changing and under construction. We can try to approach this experience of immersive participation, in a smaller way today, by learning the history of our local town or neighborhood, viewing ourselves as a continuation of its founding story.

The city, as a concept and actuality, has been used for thousands of years as a way of telling stories and myths. Let's consider just a few ways in which our ancestors thought of the cities they built, from the perspective of myth and metaphor.

The First City- Builders

Consider the creation story of ancient Mesopotamia. As probably the earliest peoples to create cities, the Mesopotamians had a dilemma on their hands; how to make sense of this completely new way of living, called civilization, which they were in a sense just making up as they went along. They turned to their gods for insight, and in the process, new myths and gods arose to give them some understanding of how to manage this new way of life.

Two fundamental creator gods in Mesopotamian religion were named Tiamat and Apsu, the Mother and Father of All. Tiamat as mother represented chaotic untamed and unknown Nature, while Apsu stood for ordered Civilization, the known, understood, and manageable. They procreated and their children too were gods; but like human children, they were noisy and disruptive. Apsu became frustrated and sought to control them, which angered the young gods to the point of rebellion, ending in the murder of their father.

Even after this horror though, the children continued to live on the corpse of their father. They relied on the order he had provided but did not respect or understand what had been supporting them, killing him and that structure in their selfish ignorance and small-mindedness. Tiamat was of course horrified that her children killed her husband, and in her wrath sent chaos upon them, in the form of an army of monsters. The young gods sought to fight back, and selected one from among themselves to lead the battle. His name was Marduk, who was victorious over the demons of chaos and essentially took on the role of his murdered father Apsu. He founded a city as a monument to himself and his victory, and from the blood of the chaotic monsters he formed the first humans. The ordered city was Babylon, populated by monstrous, chaotic humans.

What do we make of such a story? We humans have nature as our foundation, but must have a living basis of structured civilization in which to operate; a culture. Both nature and culture offer blessings and curses, and we receive both according to the respect we show. Nature provides both bounty and chaos; culture provides stable protection but can become deeply oppressive. Culture is troublesome in a way that nature is not, however; it must be constantly renewed, rethought, and updated. As much respect and deference as we must give to our ancestors, we must progress beyond them, otherwise we live on their "old dead corpse" of outmoded cultural and religious ideas. The old ways are not to be rejected so much as to be updated; that which is of value retained but incorporated in a new larger perspective. Those ancestors did the best they could, given what they knew and understood; now we must respect but improve upon that work, with deep humility and an understanding of our own shortcomings.

Lagash was one of the first of the Mesopotamian cities, and one of the most unusual. It was built on water; successive layers of mounded mud were created amongst the reed marshes between the Tigris and Euphrates Rivers; a sort of floating city. Founded perhaps 6500 years ago, it was inhabited for several thousand years. Although abandoned long ago, a few small floating villages still exist in southern Iraq. In our own contemporary experience, we know of Venice, which is also a sort of floating city. We witness today the sinking in Venice with dismay; that rational structure is sinking back into the chaotic nature of the sea, from whence it came. We can understand such a physical setting, and its process of construction and maintenance as a metaphor; our conscious human endeavors, grand as they may be, always rest upon the unknown depths of the unconscious.

Non-western Cities Built as Spiritual Metaphor

The places we build reflect the values we hold. Our furthest city-building ancestors very often built their cities with a sense that they were reflecting some sort of heavenly order upon the land. There are innumerable examples of urbanism based upon spiritual, symbolic, or metaphorical intentions. This was typically manifested in the location and orientation of a main temple and central square, and the astronomical alignment of a main street or avenue. This is normally limited to a precinct, compound, or individual building, however. Rarely has an entire city been planned and designed as a symbolic whole.

Various capital cities of empires in the Americas of course display elements of cosmological or spiritual intentions in their layout. Cities of the Mayan civilization, and Tenochtitlan, capital of the Aztec Empire show this. An amazing deviation is the layout of Cusco, the capital of the Inca Empire. Its shape was in the form of a puma, a sacred animal totem symbolic of the power of the earth.

The ancient Vedic practice of Vaastu Shastra in India is a form of geomancy, similar to Chinese Feng Shui but possibly predating it by centuries. It is a collection of principles in the service of architecture, interior design, and urbanism. These principles focus on relationship of the built environment to the cardinal directions, the five fundamental elements of nature (air, water, earth, fire, space), and astronomy. It also takes into account localized conditions of the natural environment. It is a method of creating living spaces replicating the divine cosmos. The most well-known city built upon its principles is Jaipur India. It was established in 1727 as a fully planned city, spiritually ruled by the deity Govind Dev Ji, and laid out as a mandala of nine sections, corresponding to the nine planets.

Perhaps the most intriguing example of cities fully laid out to reflect a cosmological order is to be found in China. Numerous villages and small cities are laid out in the pattern of a "bagua." The bagua is a symbol in the Taoist spiritual tradition. It symbolizes the cosmology of the Tao and the eight fundamental principles of reality or forces of nature. These are shown as the eight trigrams of the I Ching arranged octagonally around the classic yin yang symbol. A bagua is also a tool used in feng shui, a Chinese form of geomancy or design on the land.

The largest and most complete of the communities laid out in this manner is Tekes, completed in 1936 in far western China. Each of the eight main streets is 1200 meters long. Four ring roads shape the octagon, with eight radial streets within the first ring, sixteen in the second ring, thirty-two in the third and sixty-four in the outer ring. Walking these streets, one is fully immersed in a setting of spiritual reflection.

Greek and Roman Ideals

The early Greeks took the art of building cities very seriously. Socrates, one the foundational philosophers of our western heritage, said that "By far the greatest and most admirable form of wisdom is that needed to plan and beautify cities." The earliest known urban planner also was a Greek, known as Hippodamus, in the 5th century BC. Coming out of the rational Greek way of thinking, it was he who standardized the gridded arrangement of straight streets set at right angles.

The heritage of the Roman Empire was also very rational in its approach. In the layout of its cities, a central point was identified, from which two streets at right angles would emanate; the Cardo, aligned north to south, and the Decumanus running east-west. But it was not merely a rational process of engineering; once an area of land was chosen, the first step was a ceremony known as the Pomerium. This ceremony demarcated the boundaries of the city, making sacred space. It is said that Romulus conducted the Pomerium for the city of Rome in the year 752 BC, plowing the ground around the city and marking it with boundary stones.

The ancient world assumed that the gods were intimately concerned with city-building, and that a protective deity was essential to the vitality of a city. Macrobius, a Roman living in the early 400's AD, stated that, "…it is well known that every city is under the protection of some deity…". Athens was for instance overseen by Athena; the tutelary god of Rome however was kept secret upon pain of death. Cities were indeed imbued with spiritual significance, not merely economic practicality.

Medieval Europe

The medieval world, growing as it did out of the wreckage of the end of the Roman Empire, was chaotic to say the least. Towns and cities were few and far between for centuries, but slowly coalesced around centers of stability, usually castles or monasteries.

Considering European urbanism, we typically consider Rome as the most spiritually inspired city, although this physical manifestation is somewhat haphazard and uncoordinated. After the fall of the Roman Empire, the city shrank from a peak population of over one million, to perhaps as few as 17,000 inhabitants by the mid 1500's. Under Pope Sixtus V, a series of streets began to give the remaining city some coherence. These were intended to connect the seven churches within the city, as a method of improving transportation and the routes of religious pilgrims. This was essentially to connect preexisting spiritual centers; it was largely a transportation effort rather than any reflection of fully spiritual intentions.

The cities of medieval Europe were often designed, and certainly understood, in terms of spiritual metaphor. The geographer Keith Lilley states, in an article entitled Cities of God: Medieval Urban Forms and Christian Symbolism, that such symbolic form is to be found in the circle and the cross. From the 12th through 14th Centuries towns were often laid out in general terms in order to reflect the heavenly City of God. A circular wall pierced by gates located at the four cardinal points was understood as an imitation of the heavenly City of God.

The German architect Klaus Humpert has researched the layout of various medieval cities, particularly Frieburg in Germany. His findings seem to debunk the idea that the maze-like streets were "organic," natural and unplanned. Quite often they were, but such streets were very often highly intentional in their use of precise geometric lines and curves. Designers of the time were completely fascinated by numbers and used geometry as a way of being in accord with God's rules. Not only were significant buildings designed according to mathematical principles, but entire towns.

Faust and His City

One of the great treasures of western literature is Goethe's rich work, Faust. The story of Faust goes back much further than Goethe though; the theme of selling one's soul to the devil is an ancient one. Goethe was writing during the late 1700's and early 1800's, at a time of rapid decline in faith and religion amidst the rise of science and technology. It seems what Faust was doing in selling his soul to the devil was to transfer his trust from a vision of spirit to the rational mind of science and technology as his source of salvation. The story of Faust is a critique of this shift of western values.

Part Two of Faust was published in 1832, more than two decades after Part One, and it contains the story that concerns us here. In his adventures with the devil Mephistopheles, Faust is gifted a vast tract of land along the seaside. It is Faust's great desire to build a city, a powerful metropolis. In fact, the land upon which he builds is actually land reclaimed from the sea, which has been pushed back into the far distance. The city is isolated from the sea except for a canal which extends from the harbor to Faust's palace; it is used for pirate ships to bring gold and treasure to Faust.

And yet even with the fulfillment of Faust's desires, he remains deeply unsatisfied. There remains on his land a small hut and temple, the home of the elderly couple Baucis and Philemon, who will not leave. They had been granted their home years earlier by the gods Zeus and Hermes, in return for the kind hospitality the couple provided. This frustrates Faust enormously, and he seeks some way of removing them. Plans go awry and the couple are accidentally killed. This too angers Faust, who nonetheless heartlessly begins yet another urban development project, which turns out to be the death of him. What he thought was the sound of new wall foundations being constructed was the sound of shovels digging his grave.

It is generally understood that this story in the Faust saga recounts man's desire to control the world through rational means of technology, science, and engineering. Goethe perceived western civilization as having given up on its spiritual foundations, represented by the sea (metaphorically, the unconscious), seeking to rely solely on the conscious ego with all its misguided desires. While the conscious ego arises out of the unconscious (the land Faust reclaimed from the sea), it cannot do without a humble submission and connection to and respect for its source. Faust kept only one small and utterly practical relationship to the sea, the canal used to bring stolen wealth to his urban palace.

What are we modern urbanists to make of such a story? Perhaps, that a healthy civilization and its cities must maintain connection to the sea of the unconscious soul, to include it as a partner; and also, not seek to destroy the humanity of kindness and natural relationship as represented by Baucis and Philemon. Perhaps we can instead begin to imagine a city full of metaphorical canals reaching out to the soul of the sea, filled with temples of welcome and relationship.

The Contemporary American Experience

In our contemporary world here in the US, essentially no cities in our experience function in any metaphorical or inspirational manner. As a nation, we have chosen the anti-urban format of sprawling suburbia, dominated by cars. This cuts us off from that metaphorical sea of unconscious soul and nature as a whole, but also from the best of our conscious ego. In its stead we substitute comfort, predictability, and engineered convenience. There is however one very unexpected example we can draw from for a positive experience of an uplifting urban metaphor – Washington DC. The manner in which Pierre L'Enfant designed the city is one enormous spiritual metaphor, though we never imagine such a thing in a city defined by politics. With support from George Washington, who hired him in 1791, L'Enfant saw the need for the city, in its very pattern and physical layout, to symbolically reflect the values grounded in the Constitution and Declaration of Independence. This is described in the book The Sacred Geometry of Washington DC, by Nicholas Mann. Mann argues that L'Enfant's method was to make use of the symbolic meaning found in a geometric arrangement of the numbers 5 and 6. In the ancient world, Mann argues, the number 5 represented the earth and its people; to reflect this, L'Enfant created a template of five-pointed stars which determined the angles of the avenues around the US Capitol. The number 6 on the other hand, represented to the ancients the gods in heaven, the king, or in our case, the President. To symbolize that, L'Enfant created two avenues radiating out from the White House at 60-degree angles. Thus, a tension of opposites is revealed, between heavenly aspirations and earthly mechanics. The question posed to us by this urban metaphor is, how do we conduct our lives in order to manage these opposing forces, both as individuals and collectively as a people.

As we have just seen, we can say that cities grow and develop not only for various practical reasons, but also that they seem to be shaped by larger aspirations of soul as it seeks for meaning and purpose. There is some role for the city that has nothing to do with the practical needs of life. This is what I might call the "useless city." I began this chapter by stating that to understand the city and what it offers us, we must look much more deeply, to the psychology of myth and metaphor which surrounds the very idea of a city.

But what are the details we need to come to terms with? It's fine to think in generalized terms of the city as a metaphor, but a metaphor of what? What are the specifics, of myth and metaphor, of the city and the psyche, that we must become familiar with? These are elements that Jung described as archetypes. The following chapter will begin our dive into the world of Jung's archetypal thinking, and the development of what the archetypes of the city might be.

Questions to Ponder

- Did my ancestors come from a big city or small town?
- What assumptions do I hold about cities in other times and places?
- Are there mythical stories surrounding the city or town in which I live now?

CHAPTER III

Archetypal Elements of the City

"All the most powerful ideas in history go back to archetypes"—Carl Jung

Arc de Triomphe, Paris; Unattributed Photo

IN AN ATTEMPT TO MAKE USE OF, AND relate to, the city as a setting and source of psychic development, the concept of the archetypes must be considered and understood. Archetypes are a fundamental aspect of the human psyche, according to Carl Jung. Before diving in to an exploration of urban archetypes, we'll need to get a basic grounding in what archetypes represent and the role they play in the larger human unconscious. We can then begin to discover how they might be found in the urban environment, the symbolism they hold, and how we can relate to and make use of them.

Most of what the general public knows of the psychology of Jung has to do with personality type; introvert and extrovert, thinking and feeling, and so forth. This however barely scratches the surface of what his insights can provide us. His psychology is not focused so much on the elimination of neurosis in order to fit into society in a more comfortable and acceptable fashion; but for those individuals who no longer desire or are unable to, "fit in" to societal norms, and are possessed by a need to rise above convention. Jung was not so much interested in merely healing neurosis, but in connecting his patients with the numinous. Make that connection, he knew, and neurosis begins to fade away, making room for a life of meaning and purpose. This involves connecting to and building relationship with the unconscious, or what in past ages was term the Soul. In the larger context however, he provides a way of understanding large movements of the collective experience of humanity over the course of our history, ancient and contemporary.

But all that begins in the individual psyche. Jung saw that the conscious ego – that entity that each of us defines as "me" – is actually a quite small facet of the vastly larger and more complex entity he termed the Self. The Self consists of all that makes up an individual; the conscious ego, its awareness and knowledge and sense; and the vastly greater unconscious of an individual.

The Self, to reiterate, includes both conscious, which we generally understand as the personal ego, and the unconscious; all those aspects of our more complete self which we are unaware. The concept of the Unconscious has two levels. The uppermost layer is that of the personal, private, and individual, containing forgotten or repressed memories or information. The larger and deeper layer of the unconscious is that of the Collective Unconscious, which holds contents shared by all humans and are inborn or inherited. The collective unconscious is the whole of psychological life shared by all humans. This might be described as the psychological equivalent of biologically inherited instinct. So then, where do archetypes fit into such a scheme?

What Are Archetypes?

Archetypes are the contents of the collective unconscious. This collective unconscious holds all the contents that are shared by us all, common to all of humanity, and are inborn; the shared and inherited psychological life of all humans, coming down through millions of years of life experience of the species. They are in a sense the evolved structures of the collective unconscious, developed over millennia of collective lived experience.

Archetypes then are universal images existing since remotest times, grounded even in our pre-human ancestry. Think of them as aspects of our inherited psychological instincts. They are found in and transmitted by myth, fairy tales, ritual, and religion. Humans have an apparent need to create meaning out of natural events. These act as symbolic expressions of the unconscious drama of the soul. Archetypes never rise to consciousness directly, but can only be experienced indirectly, through the images of symbols, dreams, religion, art, ritual, and so forth.

The archetypes make up the evolved psychological instincts of humanity. Perhaps the following helps to explain what may have taken place. Over the course of our evolution as a social species, we acted in social ways without true awareness of what we were doing; we simply acted in particular instinctual ways because they worked well enough to support our existence. We cooperated in a respectful manner because that made life easier, essentially. This was purely instinctual, without awareness. Over the course of thousands of years, we began to re-enact those habits through ritual, as a way to re-enforce them as social norms. Upon reflection, perhaps our distant ancestors began to wonder why they operated in such fashion; in the glimmer of early yet still foggy consciousness, they created myths and stories, again to re-enforce patterns of successful behavior. Much more recently, this myth-making eventually became more formalized into high religion. What we understand today of the unconscious psyche of humanity, in our psychological approach, has in our past, always been held by religion and myth. That has always been a fundamental role of religion; yet while we now try to live without any universally accepted cultural role for religion, the underlying psychological drive to express the archetypes has not been diminished at all. When myth and religious lore is passed down through tradition, it can grow and become more comprehensive, if allowed to. But certainly, eons of tradition can smother the original experience of the archetypes. Today as always, we can recover that experience through individual spiritual practice.

Archetypes are metaphors of psychological processes and represented in various ways. Some archetypes are personified (wise old man, divine child, trickster, great mother); others are nature based (the mountain, the river, the sea, the rising sun). They are always bivalent; that is, they hold both positive and negative potential; the archetype of Mother may be nurturing but also smothering; the King archetype may be protective but also oppressive. As such, they carry emotional meaning for us; thus, while Jung identified and named the basics, they may number in the hundreds or even thousands.

What They Are Not

Archetypes are universal to all of humanity, not personal. The private individual equivalent of an archetype is the personal complex. These are restricted to an individual and not shared. A complex is a collection of thoughts, feelings, attitudes, and memories surrounding a particular idea. These live in the personal unconscious and refer to all the information and experiences of an individual's lifetime that have been forgotten or repressed but continue to influence our behavior and attitudes at an unconscious level.

The Role of Symbols, Metaphor, and Myth

The unconscious seeks to communicate with us, but it does not speak any human language. It operates instead with symbols. Symbols are therefore carriers of meaning and form a basic connection with archetypes.

It is important to distinguish between archetype, symbol, and metaphor. Metaphor is an "as if" statement; a comparison between two things. A symbol on the other hand is visual in nature, and more abstract, conveying more complex and more hidden meaning than a mere sign. Symbols are methods to convey a thought beyond what words can easily convey.

Symbols do not flow from the unconscious to tell us what we already know, but to show us what we have yet to learn. That which we seek will manifest as a symbol. They help us navigate life by providing examples – I am not alone in this situation; others have gone through this same situation throughout history. They help us realize that our personal experience is universal, that we can learn from the experience of our ancestors. They put our lives in the broader context of human history, that we participate in an ongoing story.

Joseph Campbell, a leading scholar in the fields of mythology and comparative religion, also developed four fundamentals in his field of study. He explained that myth has four basic functions: *mystical, cosmological, sociological, and pedagogical.*

1. The **mystical** function is to awaken us to the mystery and wonder of creation, to open our minds and senses to an awareness of the mystical "ground of being," the source of all phenomena.

2. The **cosmological** function is to describe the "shape" of the Universe and our world, so that it becomes vivid and alive to us, infused with meaning and significance. Every piece of creation has meaning and a role to play.

3. The **sociological** function is to pass down "the Law," the moral and ethical codes for people in a culture to follow, in order to define and support the prevailing social structure.

4. The **pedagogical** function is to lead us through particular rites of passage that define the significant stages of life, from dependency to maturity to old age to death. These rites bring us into harmony with creation and allow us to make the journey from one stage of life to another, with a sense of security and purpose.

We need to somehow relate this concept to cities and the urban pattern. We can do this by turning to the urban thinker Jane Jacobs. In her book The Death and Life of Great American Cities, she identified four basic conditions of a good city.

1. Districts must serve more than two functions so that they attract people with different purposes at different times of the day and night.

2. Blocks must be small with dense intersections giving pedestrians opportunities to interact.

3. Buildings must be diverse in terms of age and form to support a mix of low-rent and high-rent tenants. By contrast, an area with exclusively new buildings can only attract businesses and tenant's wealthy enough to support the cost of new building.

4. Districts must have a sufficient density of people and buildings.

So, Jacobs and Campbell each have identified four characteristics that are essential in their respective areas of inquiry. Do they parallel or support each other in any way? Not directly, but making big intuitive leaps is common in my thinking, leading to my reputation for mixing metaphors and torturing them until they conform. There is something here I sense, so bear with me as I wander around the possibilities...

What are the mythical, cosmological, sociological, and pedagogical possibilities of Jacobs requirements of urban design? What are the urban elements that embody a good myth? Perhaps an easier way of considering all this is to think in terms of archetypes. Archetypes, as we have seen, are recurring patterns, images, and symbols, found in religions and mythologies all over the world. It seems to me that the common theme between Jacobs and Campbell is that both good urbanism and good myths do two things; teach us and connect us. Perhaps we can think of Jacobs four qualities as fundamental archetypes of urban design.

As compelling as what Jacobs has identified however, four fundamental archetypes seem somehow insufficient. A more extensive language of urban design archetypes is needed. Christopher Alexander provides this for us, beyond the fundamentals, in his book A Pattern Language. This is the point at which the insights of Jacobs and Campbell seem to merge most fully. A Pattern Language is the practical companion to another Alexander work, The Timeless Way of Building, which provides a theoretical foundation for the patterns, or archetypes, that Alexander identifies. Alexander's pattern language includes 253 distinct elements of good urbanism and architecture. The patterns he has identified are divided into categories of Regions, Towns, Neighborhoods, Buildings, Rooms, and on down to the details of Construction. The nature of these is both practical (the proper dimensions for spacing ductwork) and wildly playful (design streets to accommodate dancing).

Rather than going through all 253 elements, I'll simply encourage you to find and enjoy the work on your own, and dive deeply into these ideas. But don't stop there... Alexander's magnum opus is a 4– volume work entitled *The Nature of Order: An Essay on the Art of Building and the Nature of the Universe*. No small vision there!

Basic Jungian Archetypes

According to Jung, there are innumerable archetypes. As carriers of meaning, there may be no end to them. They always bivalent; that is, they include a positive and negative aspect. They may be represented in a form of a person, such as the Wise Old Man, or in a more inanimate form or object such as the Great Tree or a river. They populate mythologies all over the world. Three basic mythological characters, again each of which is bivalent, include the individual (hero or adversary), nature (creative or destructive), cultural (wise king or oppressive tyrant).

Jung identified four fundamental archetypes, among dozens of others. We all experience these four and contain them within ourselves. These four basic archetypes are:

1. **The Persona:** How we present ourselves to the world. Derived from the Latin meaning "mask," it represents all the different social roles we play among various groups and social situations. The Persona acts to shield the ego from negative and painful images or experiences. It develops in childhood as we learn to behave in socially acceptable ways, to fit into expectations and norms. It is intended to contain all our primitive urges, impulses, and emotions that are not socially acceptable.

2. **The Shadow:** This exists as part of the unconscious and is composed of repressed or forgotten ideas, weaknesses, desires, instincts, and shortcomings. It contains all that is unacceptable to society and one's own morals and values. Whatever one is ashamed of and seeks to hide, such as envy, greed, hate, aggression. However, it may also contain positive attributes of which one feels unworthy. It is the dark side of the psyche, representing wildness, chaos, the unknown. We generally deny the existence of such aspects of ourselves and instead project them onto other people or groups.

3. **The Anima/Animus:** The Anima is a feminine image in the male psyche; the Animus is the equivalent masculine image in the female psyche. The animus represents the masculine characteristic in a woman, the anima represents the feminine aspects of a man. The anima/animus (together sometimes called the "syzygy") serves as the primary source for communication with the collective unconscious.

These archetypal images are based on what is found in both the personal and collective unconscious. As a divine couple, the anima and animus together represent completion, wholeness, and unification.

4. **The Self:** The Self is an archetype representing the unification of the consciousness and unconsciousness of an individual. It is represented in cultures throughout the world and history as a circle, square, or mandala. What we understand as the conscious ego is merely one small part of the larger whole known as the Self. The life-long process of discovering, developing, and harmonizing these two aspects of the Self is known as Individuation. The Self is considered equivalent to the religious understanding of the Soul. It is also equivalent to the "god-image." The Self is not God but the image through which we attempt to perceive God.

There are innumerable others. They may be personified as an individual human, or be represented by an object or natural feature; a rock, mountain, or the ocean. They are made use of and are familiar to us in such adventure movies as The Lord of the Rings. Examples are the King, or Queen; the Wise Old Man, the Great Mother, a Witch or Wizard, the Child, the Hero, the Jester or Fool, and so forth. Each of these functions as a carrier of meaning for the aspects of the human psyche.

Some Basic Archetypal Urban Elements

With all that background, we finally can arrive at the question for us to explore; what archetypes the city might hold for us. Many thinkers throughout history have viewed the city as a metaphor of the life of an individual. In what is known as his "Liverpool dream," Carl Jung provides one example. In this dream, he found himself in the city of Liverpool England. It was dark, foggy, gritty, and not at all uplifting. He wandered about with a few companions, who eventually left him alone. He then found at the center of the city a bright shining lamp under a green tree. He took the message of this dream as a signal that, dreary as a daily life can be, at the heart lies a vibrant and living soul.

The totality of the city may work as a symbolic representation of the Self, but what of the constituent aspects of the Self, those archetypes that inhabit us? How are they represented in an urban setting? Can we elaborate the metaphor in a similar way, in greater detail? Is it possible and useful to consider the constituent parts of a city or town, not just the concept of the city as a whole, as carriers of psychic meaning? What are its patterns and constructed details from which we can learn? We can easily imagine archetypes from the natural world – a tree, river, a mountain, wolf, or the sea – and the metaphorical meaning they hold; but are there elements of the built environment that carry such meaning as well? What symbolism might we find in the experience of the city? These would be comprised mainly by the physical built environment, but also social activities and situations such as festivals, homelessness, and so forth. All levels and intensities of the urban experience have potential for this; not only the grand metropolis but the small town and village, and all scales, from the regional pattern down to the design details of street furniture.

In delving into this question, I found essentially no literature specific to urbanism; the architecture of an individual building, yes, but the elements of the city seem to have been passed by. Let's consider a few basic elements of the urban environment that we experience regularly, which might hold archetypal symbolic and metaphorical meaning for us. A short list may comprise as few as Jacobs' four, perhaps as many as ten core elements of urban archetypes, followed then by dozens, perhaps even hundreds more, as Alexander proposes. What follows is by no means a comprehensive list, but a first attempt to explore the possibilities of the form, pattern, and elements that make up the psychic symbols of cities and towns.

- **The Street:** The course of one's life toward a destination. While the journey may be private, it is a shared and common experience of all. There may be numerous experiences and potential intermediate destinations along the way. What condition is it in, full of potholes or smoothly paved? Is it straight or curved?

- **The Plaza or Square:** The public commons, in which we gather with others to discuss and share ideas and concerns. Conventionally, the central plaza is the appropriate location of various civic elements such as city hall. Perhaps this may represent the collective unconscious.

- **The Intersection**: The choices of life which are regularly posed to us. Do I take this path or that? Which is more convenient or difficult?

- **The Sewer:** Perhaps the urban equivalent to the Shadow. The necessary, or at least unavoidable, but hidden location for everything unwanted and undesired.

- **The Stoplight:** Time to pause… or go. Caution! Give way to the needs of others. Beware of potential hazards. All is well, proceed toward your goal.

- **The Shopfront:** Windows and doorways along the sidewalk reveal to us those items we may need or desire as we travel through life. But the shop is a business, and what it can provide is not free. What price am I willing to pay for what I might need? While I am an individual, I am also dependent on and interconnected with others for support and survival.

- **The Library:** The collected knowledge and wisdom of the ages. A gathering place of community focused on learning from one another's experiences and insights. What does civilization have to teach? Like the plaza, this also is a representation of the collective unconscious, the striving to become conscious.

Parsing down the physical elements of the city with a little more precision can provide some unexpected tools for reflection. For instance, we can look at the distinct roles played by an avenue and a boulevard. In traditional urban design, as outlined in *The Lexicon of New Urbanism*, these two terms are not interchangeable but have differing roles to play. A boulevard is a large, high-capacity thoroughfare, typically formal and lined with large buildings, perhaps with tree-lined dividing islands, which brings a highway into the city. Its role is to "civilize" the highway between cities so that it fits comfortably into the urban setting. It brings the outer world into the city and tames it. By contrast, an avenue has a more internal role to play. Often having the same physical profile as boulevards, avenues are intended to provide high-capacity internal routes connecting prominent civic or institutional uses. An avenue might connect two prominent points of civic note within a city, such as a school and city hall, or a park and concert hall, or a commercial district with another of a more recreational character.

These two physical features of our surroundings can each be given distinct psychic metaphorical roles. A boulevard can be given symbolic meaning referring to a psychic gateway between an individual and society, or between one person and another. What do we allow into our lives from the wider world, and what do we send out from ourselves? At what speed and capacity do we allow such interaction? Do we have any boundaries in place, symbolically represented by elements such as street trees or bollards or parking lanes for instance, which help manage the flow?

The experience of an avenue by contrast, may be reflective of internal considerations. For instance, a basic psychological structure within us, in Jung's terms, is what is known as the "ego-self axis." This refers to a basic need for healthy psychic life and personal development in the form of a good working relationship between the conscious ego and the larger unconscious self. An avenue then can play the role of this axis, the connection of ego and self. When we become aware of traveling along an avenue, we might remind ourselves to tend to this interior relationship, between one's conscious ego and all the various archetypal components that lie within the self. How do my various emotions, values, and assumptions relate to one another, we might ask ourselves? Are there some potholes along my avenue/ axis between some element of darkness and of light which need to be repaired?

Making Use of Urban Archetypes

Archetypes exist which speak to every phase and aspect of human life; being raised as a dependent child, exploring the world, operating in society, taking on social responsibilities, preparation for death, and so on. Archetypes can assist us in finding appropriate responses to such typical and recurring human situations.

The experience of archetypes occurs through projection, and the images in which they are cloaked. These include religion, mythology, symbols, and rituals. To clarify, the term projection means to place some psychic element outside of oneself and out onto the world; another person is "good" or "bad," not me. That animal represents spiritual power, this ritual empowers me, etc., rather than accepting that goodness, badness, and empowerment all lie within me. Projection moreover, is not in any way a conscious process. We do not project directly or intentionally; rather, projection happens to us, arising unbidden from the unconscious. To overcome this however takes conscious and intentional effort.

Consider not only the physical elements of place, but the other inhabitants of your town or neighborhood. Each person you pass by on the sidewalk holds the potential to represent some aspect or your inner psyche. The homeless person, the playful child, on and on. Get to know who those "inner citizens" are. You are not just the one individual ego that you are aware of; there is a whole urban population of characters living within your unconscious.

A basic value of understanding and working with archetypes is that this helps put our lives into perspective. We are able to understand that we are participating in a wider story; all of humanity shares these stories, thus my experience, while personal, is at the same time universal. This helps shape and direct our manner of living. This awareness of archetypal patterns enables us to overcome getting stuck as the victim of these enormously powerful archetypal patterns, and we gain greater control of life with this expanded vision. They are fundamental to the process of becoming psychologically whole. The goal, in Jung's terms, is not perfection but wholeness.

Can we make the concept of "projection" an intentional, purposeful effort? Well, not really, but is there another way of considering this? Is a metaphor a sort of conscious projection? As an "as if" statement? I think it is safe to say that the majority of people associate the city with all sorts of negative traits, that is, many tend to project fear and negativity onto the city. To overcome this, we must seek the symbols and create the metaphors that lie there, waiting to reveal themselves.

The elements of the city are more than mere functional objects in the cityscape. They can play the same role as the Stations of the Cross in traditional catholic church sanctuaries; as teaching aids for our process of self-reflection and psychic development.

Let's back up a little here, and consider something quite unexpected. One purpose of this search to uncover the archetypes of urbanism is to bring to consciousness the aspects of what Jung called the "religious function." A bold concept on my part, to be sure. First, a definition of what meant by this term is needed. Jung saw that humans have an inherent desire and capacity – an instinct, we could call it – to experience the sacred, to connect with a higher power, and seek meaning beyond the personal self. What we understand today of the unconscious and its contents in a psychological way has always, until about the last 250 years or so, been held by religion. That has been the larger purpose of religion; a tool with which we can interact with the archetypes. We have lost touch with this capacity over the last several hundred years since the Enlightenment, with the rise of logical rational thinking and the scientific method. Our increasingly rational technocratic way of thinking has pushed down into the unconscious this irrational yet fundamental aspect of humanity, where it remains unheeded. It occasionally pops back out in unhealthy ways, such as distorted politics.

We must be able to interact with these unconscious elements of ourselves. Finding their meaning in the physicality of the city or town that surrounds us is a useful tool in the growth and healing process. Can our interaction with the archetypes of urbanism act as a sort of retrieval of the religious function? This is not a call for a return to traditional religion, nor an attempt to turn the physical city as some fetishistic object of worship. Rather, this is an effort to develop a new tool for communicating with the soul.

Archetypes lie dormant in the unconscious, waiting for an opportunity to manifest themselves. Think of them as a dry riverbed, waiting to be filled once again with the water of life. Archetypal energy must be channeled to become manifest. They can become unmoored over time, restless and no longer satisfied to flow within the prevailing riverbed of cultural patterns and religious systems. As the waters of life expand over the centuries – that is, as our concepts and detailed understanding of the world expand – the old riverbed becomes inadequate to channel all the increased water of expanded psychic energy. Today, those waters are overflowing the banks of the 2,000-year-old river of Christianity, so to speak. Understanding the city as a natural setting for spiritual quest can be a method of widening those riverbanks, creating a larger container for the ever more energetic archetypes to flow.

I think of religion as a socialized starter-kit for those on private spiritual quest. Cultural religions and their accompanying moral and cosmological teachings are filled with images, myths, and insights, all collected over the centuries, from which an individual may begin their private spiritual journey, which essentially involves delving into, and building relationship with, both the personal and collective unconscious. I sense most of us have irrevocably left traditional religion behind, yet the psychological yearning it helped fulfill remains. Its traditional metaphors and symbols no longer speak to us, and we are in need of new ones. At the same time, we are becoming an increasingly urban world. While nature taught us for thousands of years, providing the material for the archetypes to develop, we no longer have a daily experience of the natural world. Ours is now a human-made, urban experience. We need to, in a sense, redeem the city by allowing its archetypes to speak to us. In this way the city, our collective souls, and our individual psychic experiences can be healed.

Questions to Ponder

- What other or secondary urban archetypes ought to be included?

- What non-physical elements of the urban experience might be appropriate?

- What aspects of the city hold symbolic meaning for you?

CHAPTER IV

The City as a Classroom: Spiritual Development and Psychic Exploration

"It is good for the soul to nurture relationships with places as well as with people" —Thomas Moore

Friendship Arch, Chinatown; Washington, D.C.

Our understanding of the city, it purposes and relationship to the larger world, has changed significantly over time and from one civilization to another. While there are numerous examples of cities designed to reflect some cosmological vision, or used intentionally as a setting for ritual, what we are exploring in this book is the process of using the city as the intentional setting for personal growth and insight. Experiencing the city as a worthy setting gives the soul a greater vocabulary, new material to work with, providing it with images and scenarios and memories to make use of when it wants to communicate with us in a dream or other interaction. To observe and reflect on the life of the city is to observe and reflect on one's inner life.

Incarnation on Earth: A Boarding School Experience

Our essential being is spirit, temporarily inhabiting matter. Think of us all as incarnated spirits, temporarily here on earth as humans; basically, a group of struggling students sent to a boarding school. A well-known quote attributed to the Aboriginal tribes of Australia, phrases this well: "We are all visitors to this time, this place, just passing through. Our purpose here is to observe, learn, grow, and love. Then we return home." We are sent here to learn lessons, and the pedagogical tool used is experience. This is incredibly difficult; as Oscar Wilde put it, "Experience is the hardest teacher. It gives the exam first and the lesson later." Or, from Eckhart Tolle, "We are here to experience… limitation." I would add that we are also to awaken from unconsciousness and discover the opportunities and obligations of conscious self-awareness.

So, experiencing life on earth is our schooling. For some it is elementary school, others graduate school, for some unfortunates it is reform school, all jumbled together in the same class; and we all return until the lessons are learned and integrated. Much of the personal spiritual growth that is intended for us takes place unconsciously, but we are best served when this spiritual journey is made conscious with intentionality. The physical places in which we locate ourselves therefor have a significant impact on our opportunities for spiritual growth and what lessons become available to us. If this physical world is the "school" to which we are all sent, we have a large responsibility to provide the most advantageous, well-organized and supplied classrooms possible. This means creating places of grace, beauty, memory, opportunity, connection, and interaction. Our current image of urbanism, as little more than a set of engineered infrastructure in support of real estate investment opportunities, is profoundly inadequate for such a task and must be shattered.

Such a view of incarnation assumes the possibility of re-incarnation. Is this not a sort of "spiritual evolution?" A refinement of soul over generations of time. This should not come as such a great surprise to those of us raised in the Christian west; the Christian world itself held to the idea of re-incarnation for its first 500 years. A city grows, changes, and matures in the same way. Over time, a place, either natural or built, can become infused with meaning. City-building is essentially about the creation of meaning… I am in *this* place, connected to the ideas it represents and the stories that took place here. Meaning may be arbitrary and highly personal, yet it is essential to a fulfilled life. A city or town or village is more than its physicality, and more too than the people who inhabit it. It is an entity unto itself, which our ancestors birthed, and we nurture and inhabit. It is a living chakra in a sense, a series of nodes of living energy.

A fundamental task of humanity is to discover the eternal by experiencing the temporal. The eternal is interpreted and discovered through myth and metaphor. In our experience of temporal urbanism, that which is eternal or transcendent is understood and shared via symbols, rituals, and art. As spirits now physically incarnated into this world, we are like scouts or explorers sent out to discover some new undiscovered territory; it is the scout's duty to gain as much understanding as possible and report back what has been learned. The conscious ego that I recognize as "me" is the scout, only a small part of a much larger entity of my Self, which transcends time and space. Perhaps we can say then that the merging of spiritual quest and urban experience anticipates what Jung viewed as the next phase in human psychic development, the reconciliation of opposites. An extraordinarily complex task to be sure, requiring the ability to confront that which we would rather avoid. But, to paraphrase Jung, there is no coming to maturity without relationship to one's environment. This sort of deep relationship and interdependence must now include more than only the natural world; rock and river and tree; but the built world of street, building, and plaza as well. But what does that really entail?

A New Perspective on Nature

We absolutely must learn to think of the city as an aspect of nature. Granted, we have been incredibly inept at designing and outfitting our cities for several generations, so the assumption that cities are a terrible and ugly affront to nature is perfectly understandable. But our built environment is only a reflection of the values we hold, neither of which seem worthy now. Change our values, change our cities. We learn and discover ourselves by the experience of a city. First though, we need to understand the context of the city; its setting in a relationship with the natural world.

A conventional understanding of nature for a contemporary American is expressed as pristine wilderness untouched by humanity. This consists of green woodlands, furry creatures, rivers and lakes, seaside and mountains, all imbued with positive traits of beauty and goodness. Usually stones and rocks are included in such a perspective as well, but for the most part, nature is thought of as the grand and beautiful. This represents the outlook of western thinking of only the last several generations, which splits nature and humanity apart. This understanding of nature is a fairly recent outlook and is by no means universal in human experience. A comprehensive vision of "nature" is needed that includes human creations. The city can no longer be viewed as something apart from nature. We often need to escape the city and dive into field and forest as a refuge from too much civilization—the concept of "forest bathing" has recently appeared. But would it not be better to create an urbanism from which no escape is needed? The term "paradise" means "walled garden" - so paradise assumes living in culture and nature joined together.

Nature is not "free" in a way that we are not; we humans are not trapped or enslaved by some nefarious demonic force. I would argue just the opposite; we humans are the ones made free, through our consciousness, severely limited and abused though it is; it is nature which is trapped. A dog or cat is limited to being a dog or cat; a tree must be a tree and nothing else. It can do nothing but obey the laws of chemistry, physics, and inherited biology. What we envy in them is their relative lack of consciousness, and their corresponding lack of responsibility. But we are conscious, giving us both opportunity and responsibility. Our failing is an inability or unwillingness to fully take on these opportunities and responsibilities.

What is "nature?" A dictionary definition of the term "nature" is fairly all-encompassing: "The phenomenon of the physical world collectively, including plants, animals, the landscape, and other features and products of the earth, as opposed to human creations." The popular imagination seems more specific; when we say we want to go relax in nature, we typically envision lots of beautiful and calming scenery, absent the unexpected dangers that nature always presents. Our thinking about nature seems much too narrow; perhaps this is because it is an idea, a human invention. One way of narrowing down what "nature" includes lies in deciding what is not natural. Well, what does that encompass, other than things that are man-made? Everything. The follow-up question is, why are man-made things not natural? Are humans not part of nature?

All creatures have instinct, including humans; but what we additionally possess is conscious intentionality. Perhaps this intentionality is the source of our suspicion against ourselves. Our intentions can be equally injurious or supportive. A frog does not have to decide what it means to be a frog; a human, however, has the possibility- even a requirement, an obligation I would say- to determine what a human life can be. How we decide that question has enormous implications.

Is nature limited to planet Earth? Were the Apollo astronauts in "nature" when walking on the moon? Is the Kuiper Belt at the outer reaches of the solar system part of nature? This is certainly not an environment we were physically designed for, nor is the Marianas Trench at the bottom of the ocean. What we must consider as part of nature is not always pleasant or appropriate. However we define nature, we feel disconnected from it, from something fundamental that we should – by nature – have a strong and vibrant relatedness with. But we don't. A split in thinking has taken place.

Nature has not always been loved. Over the centuries, differing cultures have had different views. Those people and cultures most intimate with "nature" have a greater respect for the dangerous destructive powers within the natural environment than those of us in the contemporary western world, protected as we are by all the accoutrements of civilization. For many if not most ancient cultures, nature was dominated by a dark and dangerous aspect. The city is the last place we contemporary westerners think of when considering "nature," but it has often been understood as a safe refuge from the dangers of chaotic wilderness. Followers of the Judeo-Christian heritage will recall that the Old Testament reviles the city as a dangerous evil... up to a point. After the Israelites wandered the desert wilderness for 40 years, they built themselves a refuge; a city, Jerusalem.

A full understanding of urbanism must consider the separation we feel from nature. To the extent we feel such isolation, it is self-induced by having turned "nature" into an idea filled with cultural assumptions and parameters. Two of our approaches to thinking about nature and our separation from it strike me as most significant. The first regards what we seem to hope to find in a connection to "nature." Nature is foundational of course, but is it always good and positive? Not to the gazelle about to be snared by the lion, nor the deer buried under a storm-induced mudslide. What we consider nature is not always kind or beautiful. Its systems operate without any apparent regard to outcomes. Perhaps then what we seek is not nature itself, but its beauty. The Jungian psychologist James Hillman has stated this most clearly; the split we experience is not between the human and natural worlds, but in what humans are seeking. While we certainly belong to nature – it has been our home forever – it is not nature in itself that we desire today, but the beauty it contains. This is the beauty of non-human forms of being alive that we sense in a tree, a bee, an elk. The rolling flow we see in clouds overhead or the ever-changing-yet-always-the-same tumble of water in a rushing river reminds us of the life within ourselves. This connection with the beauty inherent in life is what we seek; nature then becomes the vehicle rather than the destination.

A further connection we desire, along with beauty, is the creative act which nature represents. Living nature is creativity unleashed in unimaginable, ever-evolving ways. Traditional cultures have understood that the creativity of life is not limited to the world of plants and animals. Human artifacts can be imbued with life as well, such as totems, icons, talismans, and other ritual objects. This is why certain works of art move us so deeply; they are containers of soul. Our contemporary worldview of excessive rationality has killed the "alive-ness" of human artifacts, however. Objects can no longer have soul to the rational western mind. We suffer from too much rationality.

The second break with nature we have forced upon ourselves is a split between living, green, or organic nature, from what I think of as "structural nature." These are two aspects of the same thing, yet we tend to disregard the structural. When I speak of living nature, I am envisioning those green, organic aspects of creation; animal and vegetable, which exhibit active life, as well as water and wind, whose movements and motion can also give a sense of life. How do we integrate living nature into the urban environment? More than a few writers and designers with greater skill than mine, have explored this extensively. The most obvious is the inclusion of street trees. A well arrayed network of connected parks, large and small, both active and passive, is a universally positive aspect of any successful modern city.

Various technical means of incorporating green nature into urbanism are gaining prominence. First, a new method in the way we manage stormwater is becoming more widespread. The process known as "daylighting" involves bringing back into the open a river or stream that had been buried and channeled into sewer pipes. Green roofs, planted with grasses and shrubs, are a second technical method of bringing more green life into urban settings. These view water as a resource to be cared for rather than a problem to be quickly dispensed with. Community gardens and other agrarian approaches to greening the city bring organic locally sourced food production help structure neighborhoods and nurture both people and nature.

Yet there are elements of the physical environment which are not "alive" in the conventional sense, yet still exhibit dynamic movement. We experience this in the flow of a river, billowing clouds, the shifting of entire continents due to plate tectonics. Our love of nature must include more than a desire to be surrounded by greenery and cute furry animals, but to be in harmony with these systems and patterns as well. An example of such patterns is described by the "Rule of 15%" as revealed by Geoffrey West, in his book, Scale. His research has found that for every doubling in the size of a city's population, the cost of infrastructure increases by only 85%, while socioeconomic elements such as income and crime also increase by 15%. This is similar to the "Quarter Power Rule," or Kleiber's Law which governs living organisms, stating that for every doubling in size, the members of a species require only a 75% increase in metabolic rate. This implies that the urban pattern follows laws of nature just as living species do.

Such systems, patterns, and tendencies, I describe as the structural aspect of nature. The image that helps me make the most sense of this is that of a garden trellis. The rules, patterns, systems, and structures of nature act as a trellis or skeletal foundation upon which the living green side of nature can then manifest, grow, and flourish. This trellis is less physical than conceptual. It can be understood through geometry, mathematics, and statistics, for instance. It is found in proportions such as the Golden Mean (the ratio of 1:1.614) and Pi (the number 3.14159). Nature seems to find certain patterns and proportions more useful than others; and we find them not only useful but beautiful too.

We must therefore think of the city as an aspect of nature. In our thinking about the "nature" of nature, perhaps we are experiencing a misalignment of imagination. The fundamental images we conjure for ourselves regarding the natural world may themselves need to be questioned. A new metaphor is needed to give us better clarity.

The ideal that we set for what we consider natural is perhaps too pure, too unattainable. That ideal is the concept of wilderness. The image we have of wilderness – of land untouched by any human presence – is no longer appropriate. At this point in history, there really is very little pure wilderness left on the planet. Humans have had their impact on almost every single corner of the earth. Plastic residue is found in the deepest ocean depths, global warming is reshaping Antarctica. Indeed, human intervention is now required to maintain even a minimal level of untouched landscape; the seemingly passive goal of leaving wilderness alone now requires an intentional act. For better or worse, because of our impacts on the landscape, we have an increasingly profound obligation to manage both the land and our interactions with it.

This can only be achieved by the most difficult task, that of changing our assumptions and habits of thinking. The ideal of "wilderness" assumes – with good cause, I must admit – that every human action is negative. That leaves us little room for error unfortunately, and a reduced capacity to participate in a connection to nature. A better way of imagining the land is not through the lens of untouched wilderness, but of the garden. A garden provides a place of nurturing relationship for people. It acts as a reconciling space between the seemingly opposing values of wild nature and human creativity. A garden can be thought of as a mandorla or vesica piscis in this way, the point of reconciliation between opposing forces. When we think of a garden, we come into relationship with the land as caretakers; given our horrific mistreatment of the land for so many generations, this is a critical aspect of healing. The ways in which we interact with this global garden varies of course, with the level and type of activity. This is crucial because while many preservationists rightly condemn haphazard urban development, the opposite is equally dangerous. Haphazard preservation is just as problematic because it then forces random haphazard development.

It is easy enough to visualize the manner in which living organic "green" nature is incorporated with trees and parkland into urban settings. How is the "structural" side of nature reflected in urbanism? The basic layout of the street and block pattern, infrastructure, building types, transportation systems, take on this role, including the manner in which these are in harmony with geometry and the Law of 15% among others. The elements and physical patterning of human urban places form the structural aspect of nature, creating a trellis upon which the living green side of nature can then manifest, grow, and flourish. In discovering the manner in which a city or town can best reflect both the organic and structural aspects of nature – in asking the land itself what pattern is right for that specific place – urban design then becomes a type of geomancy.

Healing the damage we have inflicted on the land must account for the damage we have inflicted on cities as well. This of course entails healing ourselves, and this requires a new mindset. Thinking of both nature and urbanism as sacred space is a core aspect of this. How is this reflected in urbanism? Two similar terms reflect this sacred understanding of place. The ancient Celtic concept of the Nemeton, a sacred grove in a forest, reflects sacred nature. The Greek term Temenos refers to the sacred plaza in front of or surrounding a temple, is the urban equivalent of sacred space. We must learn to think of the whole of the city as a sacred Temenos.

An unexpected way of experiencing nature, whether in forest or city, is taking a deep dive into the unconscious, through meditative practices and what Jung terms "active imagination," the conversation with the soul. When these various components of nature are considered together, the urban setting is then seen as absolutely a part of "nature." But whereas both the living and structural components of nature operate purely through dynamic instinct and laws, the human psyche adds the much more complex layer of intentionality. In his Dream Analysis Seminar, Jung speaks to this in his typically unexpected way; that the meditative process itself is a way of experiencing nature. Too much civilization makes us "dirty," and we must be cleansed by connecting with nature. This might be a walk in the woods, or a bath in the sea; but equally from within, by entering the unconscious, entering oneself through dreams and meditation. This is touching nature from the inside.

In Hillmans understanding of beauty, and Jung's idea of meditation as a method of interacting with nature, we then can see that nature often functions more as a vehicle for us than as the final destination. Perhaps then we might be better off with a more wholistic perspective; rather than thinking of ourselves as passively within Nature we are actively a part of Creation.

One final approach to understanding the distinctions and connections between nature and urbanism may be helpful here. Nature is that which lies outside culture. Nature represents the unknown; culture is comprised of what we know and understand. Civilization—culture— is a limited domain of competence, while nature is an unlimited domain of mystery. Ironically, this is of course a culturally derived understanding! In the perspective of the ancient world of the near East, the unknown and unmanageable chaos of nature was represented by the Mother– what we might now call the Matriarchy— while the rationally systematized order of civilization was represented by the Father, or Patriarchy. Both provide danger and security in equal measure; Mother Nature feeds and nurtures us but her storms can destroy us just as easily; the ordered Patriarchy of civilization can protect us but also becomes horrifically oppressive and violent. They must be valued and respected equally, balanced appropriately, which we have not been doing for quite a few centuries.

Psychologically speaking, learning and growth occur by confronting the dangerously unknown and mysterious: strangers, disease, disappointment, death. These are not just found out in the wild, lying just beyond the light of the campfire. Are such unknowns not also found in an urban setting? That too is nature in the city. A core intent of psychic growth is to bring our vast mysterious unconscious contents into the light of conscious understanding. Our task is to increase our range of competence, familiarity with, and acceptance of the unknown. Or to put it metaphorically, to bring nature into the city.

A Stage for the Senses

On November 23, 534 BC, Thespis appeared onstage wearing a mask in the role of Dionysus. This made him, according to Aristotle and others, the first actor ever; that is, the first human to take to the stage as a character other than himself. Previously, all performances were either storytelling or musical and choral productions.

The ancient rituals and celebrations that our ancestors reveled in, from prehistoric tribal dances around a small fire to medieval mystery plays, continue down to this day. We see this take place in the Mummers Parade in Philadelphia and of course Mardi Gras. New Orleans seems to practically organize its life around Second Line parades. These sorts of celebrations and dramas have the ability to define a city.

The ancients made use of ritual in attempts to affect events in the outer world. Today, we need ritual to affect change in our personal inner worlds. I first learned the value of ritual through my experience growing up in the Episcopal Church. In young adulthood, I was able to compare that complex ritualistic experience with that of the Mennonites, for whom elaborate ceremony is intentionally avoided and thus almost completely lacking. And yet even they cannot fully rid themselves of something so basic to human experience. The participation in ritual, whether elaborate or plain and simple is a fundamental human desire, even a need. For us, ritual is how the seen and unseen serve one another.

When my children were young, I tried explaining to them what was happening during the Episcopal church services we attended. The first half of the service, we listen to stories, I told them. The second half, we participate in the re-enactment of a story. At ages five and seven, they just were not interested in what I tried to get across. Perhaps they have some semblance of appreciation now; that ritual, whether religious or secular, set in a church, sports stadium, or concert hall, brings meaning and therefore direction into our lives.

The psychotherapist James Hillman has indicated that young males in particular have a fundamental need for ritual in order to mature properly. We see this most clearly in the victory celebrations of competitive team sports for instance, and the military. In general society however, we have dropped most rituals as being naïve, meaningless, or manipulative. Perhaps this loss is a source of the anger, frustration, and angst we see in adolescent males today in America.

Rituals, in their social and public aspect, need a setting in which to be performed. Except for older and larger cities, civic space has become hard to find in the US. As an example, after winning the World Series, the Anaheim Angels naturally wanted to hold a victory celebration. The story, perhaps more apocryphal than true, is that there being no city square or plaza for such an event, the victory parade was held on the Main Street of Disneyland, followed by a rally in a parking lot. A contrasting approach to the design of civic space is given by Christopher Alexander, who in his book A Pattern Language, suggests that streets be designed to accommodate dancing. To give Disney their due however, the appeal of the Main Street USA setting does just that; their land planners operate as stage designers, and clearly understand better than most that the city street is intended for festive public display. This is why the Main Street USA setting in Disneyland remains one of the most popular tourist attractions in America. We enjoy it so much because we cannot enjoy anything like it back home.

Nature is its own stage for its own performance. Much as we must have a deep connection with the vibrancy of green living nature, it somehow isn't sufficient for humans. We have an inescapable desire – need – to create. We must create not only the performance but the stage on which we act. This need demands to be both expressed and experienced through the senses.

As biological creatures, we have evolved a set of senses with which to take in and interpret the world around us. As spiritual beings, these senses give us the opportunity to experience and savor that world and give it meaning. This sensing life is not unchanging though; we develop the skills to make use of it; and the senses are foundational to higher development. The urban thinker Louis Mumford stated in his Culture of Cities that "the daily education of the senses is the elemental groundwork of all higher forms of education." The experience of the city is the immersive environment so well suited to this education; he felt that the medieval town in particular was an "omnipresent work of art." What are some of the ways the various senses take in the city?

- **Sight:** We humans are an extremely visual species. About 90% of the sensory input we receive is visual, and two thirds of our brain activity is given over to the interpretation of visual stimuli. Does what we see indicate danger or safety? Does it delight us or worry us? Those things we interpret as safe and delightful we consider to be beautiful. We desire both ordered pattern and unexpected whimsy, and we find this in color, texture, and motion. These are the elements of the built environment, both in the permanent and intentional design of place, and the temporary and playful ways people make use of space.

- **Sound:** The city is usually thought of as full of the irritating noise of trucks and construction, which cannot be denied. Yet the sounds of a city can delight as well. The splashing of a fountain, chattering of children, the snippets of conversation overheard on a sidewalk. Formal and organized concerts are scheduled in parks and plazas; but more random music is sometimes available too. Recently, there emerged a movement among cities to randomly scatter pianos on sidewalks and corners, available for anyone to make impromptu music.

- **Smell:** Like sound, the smell of a city is historically a negative in the public imagination. The rise of coffee shops and roasters is combating this admirably though. So too are small artisanal bakeries, and restaurants with sidewalk seating. The smell of an artist's paint outside a gallery provides an unexpected and unusual addition to the palette of city sensory experience.

- **Taste:** How do we taste a city? Food has become an enormous driver in urban revitalization efforts. This is found not only in sidewalk cafes and outdoor restaurant seating, but particularly with food trucks roaming the streets and gathering near pedestrian centers. In larger cities, the tradition of small vendors on the street, selling roasted chestnuts and pretzels, continues. The latest twist to all this is the banana bike, traveling around the streets of Seattle and Washington DC, passing out free bananas, courtesy of a corporate sponsor.

- **Touch:** The most obvious element of a city is its collection of buildings. We touch these constantly, at least when we grab the door handle when we enter. Some buildings seem to invite touch in their use of materials or unusual shape. Street furniture, particularly benches, are absolutely made to be touched. Every aspect of the built environment has been touched by someone. Someone laid the brick, poured the concrete, planted the trees. To the extent we interact with the city in a playful, thoughtful, artistic touch, the spirit of those artisans and workers gives life to us. But we touch not only with our hands; the one aspect of any city which we simply cannot avoid touching is the sidewalk. Normally so humble, a good sidewalk may delight with color, a playful pattern in its brick or stone. It can also be the canvas upon which a memorial can be created, as in the "Extra Mile" series of bronze markers located in the sidewalks of downtown Washington DC. Even manhole covers give opportunity for art.

- **Time:** The forgotten sense that we all share is that of time. This connects us not only to the past but ought to remind us to pay attention to the future as well. Our ancestors gifted us with so much; what will we leave for our descendants? We must make sure what we provide them is worthy. Time is experienced through the cycles of days and seasons. A city will memorialize time through festivals and rituals repeated through the years. Most people will gain a sense of the spiritual in an urban setting through art festivals, music, spectacle, etc., where all the senses are put into play. The more day-to-day method of staying connected to the past in a city is, of course, the retention and re-use of old buildings. A more subtle way though, might be the honoring of ruins; older buildings and structures *not* put to our economic service but kept anyway, as reminders and teachers.

Such memorable experiences create place out of mere location. We expand our souls this way, in our interaction with the soul of place. We grow beyond the limits of our time and place, by digging more deeply into this particular time and this place.

Cities and Storytelling

Humans are at heart storytellers. Why are stories important to us? Beyond simple entertainment, they are the original educational tools. As Mr. Rogers tells us, "Frankly there isn't anyone you couldn't learn to love if you knew their story." How do we go about this? Well, it helps to be near others; and urban environments, whether city of empire or simple small village, have always offered the perfect setting to create those relationships.

One of the basic emotional needs we have is to be heard and understood by the people most important to us. We want our personal story to be heard and accepted. When we are denied this, all sorts of psychic and spiritual wounds are inflicted. Moreover, stories are a key to expanding our circle of empathy, a basic aspect of psycho/ spiritual development. These personal stories, while private and individual, are part of a larger collective narrative, repeated millions of times over the centuries. Seemingly small and insignificant at times, our little private stories are actually epic in nature.

For a succinct perspective on this, we can turn to Shakespeare to discover why cities exist; in his simple line he reminds us, "all the world's a stage." Cities provide us the best settings to tell our stories. There are all sorts of venues a city normally provides us for storytelling, whether we are on the stage or in the audience. Concert halls, libraries, opera houses, lecture halls, college auditoriums, art museums, church sanctuaries, the humble coffee shop. A classic stage for storytelling though, is one not thought of as such; the sidewalk and street corner. This informal setting is the most common stage on which we find ourselves, chatting with friends while walking or during chance encounters with acquaintances or random strangers. Some sidewalk locations are so well situated for finding an audience that chance encounters become semi-formalized. Centuries ago, London instituted a specific spot for the telling of stories, known as Speakers Corner. Since the 1700's, anyone has had the right to set up a soapbox and speak their mind to whatever audience cares to stop and listen. An urban setting then, whether grand metropolis or small town, provides us with excellent settings for hearing and telling our personal stories.

But a city does more than provide us with a larger audience to hear our story; a city also has a story to tell us. Ancient cities were often laid out as the physical reflection of some cosmological or spiritual order; an attempt to recreate heaven on earth. Dozens of cities in ancient cultures—Mayan, Aztec, Chinese, Egyptian, Indian—show patterns reflective of cosmological or cultural belief systems. Like participating in an elaborate religious ceremony, residents might have had the daily sense of being immersed in, and participating in, a grand mythological story. Perhaps surprisingly, even Washington DC was designed with such a pattern in mind. Simply being in a significant place, walking down the street, can provide the opportunity to participate as an actor in a story or play. The ancient Andean city of Tiahuanaco in Bolivia built over 1,000 years ago, seems to have been designed expressly for this purpose. It seems to have acted almost solely as a tourist attraction, an expression of the empire's cosmic significance. The builders seem to have intentionally kept the place unfinished, constantly changing and under construction. We can try to approach this immersive participation today by learning the history of our local town or neighborhood, viewing ourselves as a continuation of its founding story.

A city functions as both Archetype and Dreamscape. A city and its inhabitants tell each other their stories. Most epic stories throughout history, certainly the great ancient mythologies, have their origins in our unconscious, and come to us primarily through dreams and works of art. Can the experience of a city provoke the unconscious to speak to us in this fashion? I would say yes. If we consider the city as a classroom populated by our fellow "students of life," as a resource for the writing of our own story, and also view the city as having a story of its own to tell us, we find a new source of inspiration and growth. Since epic stories rise from the unconscious, we can liken the city to the collective unconscious, and its inhabitants to the personal unconscious. The city provides various stages for individuals to tell their stories of their personal unconscious. In turn, inhabitants of the city provide an audience to which the city can present its story, the collective unconscious common to all humanity.

We write and live out our personal stories in the places we live, whether that be city, town, village, or suburb. We imprint onto certain places our memories of meaning. I attended an uplifting concert here, a joyful reunion with a friend happened there, my child attended that school, I lost a lover there. We define ourselves partly by our relationship to place; we love or hate a place because of memory, much of which may be unconscious. Some memories fade simply because of time, others are repressed because they evoke pain. And just as memory can fail or not be as accurate as we hope, so too do places change.

Stories we tell from our personal narratives form chapters, or perhaps more accurately sub-plots, of the larger story of the collective unconscious seen in the epic of the city. We can think of urban form as a metaphorical labyrinth, through which we can process our personal story, meditating upon the images we find while walking the streets. What goes on down that alley? That building is beautiful and important; perhaps I should explore it. I need to cross this intersection to reach that restful park. Who are those people gathered over there? Urban form can provoke such little questions in us, and in turn dreams are provoked from these little scenes. Some of what will be shown to us through such urban stories will be beautiful, some not; we should accept and be grateful, for it all; ugliness and beauty are both inescapable teachers.

Beyond our individual stories, a city, whether thousands of years old or only ten, has a story of its own to tell. The story of a place includes specifics of both time and place, some of which is universally transcendent. The story comes to us in various ways such as traditions, annual festivals, parades, local legends of the people who came before us. We can think of these as the acting out of dreams.

Dreams are the vehicle by which the unconscious, both the personal and collective, speaks to us. Dreams seem odd to us, and can be hard to interpret, because the unconscious speaks a much older, non-verbal language which our conscious self then must interpret. And so, we hold festivals of art, food, dance, music, parades, and costumes to help us interpret unknown mysteries.

How does the city speak to us, and how do we speak back to the city? The city and its inhabitants provide content for each other's stories. The city and the collective unconscious it represents teaches us the bigger picture, the larger stories of what they aspire to, through our dreams; we in turn shape the city with the inspiration it gives. In this way the conscious and unconscious affect each other, a two-way conversation. But what comes to us through dreams will have a will and destiny of its own that our mere conscious selves can only blindly fight against or follow faithfully. The latter always proves the right path.

There is a narrative arc to storytelling which we can discover in urban space. The outline of the great story of human experience does not seem to ever change, though the details vary over time and place. This great story has been dubbed The Hero's Journey by the writer of comparative mythology, Joseph Campbell. This journey includes six elements, forming a narrative arc for any adventure story. These include The Call, the Road of Trials, the Abyss, Transformation, Apotheosis, and The Return.

In trying to work out what the narrative arc of urbanism might look like, I toyed with the concept of the Urban Transect – a gradient of intensity – but felt that assumed too obviously that all stories are reflected in a particular pattern of transition; your story isn't complete unless you finish in the heart of downtown, which I'm not convinced is true. In any arrangement of such an arbitrary attempt though, the storyline for the mythologizing of urbanism will include both physical aspects of design as well as situational/ cultural elements. What I provide here is of course an incomplete set of ideas and relationships. Each of us will have a different take on the ways urban experience and personal myth relate to one another. A basic and obvious one is the act of walking down the street as reflective of progressing along an inner spiritual journey. What follows is my attempt to find parallels between Campbell's classic "monomyth" and their elements, below which are my thoughts on what some possible urban equivalents could include. No doubt each reader will find others to add.

- **Call to Adventure:** Disruption, awakening, refusal of the call, finding a mentor
    - *Gateways:* Airport, train or bus station, highway exit ramp

- **Road of Trials:** Tests, expansion of vision, synchronicity
    - *Streets:* Intersections, dark alleyways, signage, lighting, crosswalks, maps

- **The Abyss:** Belly of the whale, temptation, meeting the angry god/goddess, revelation
    - *Abandonment:* Blight, political stalemate, garbage, sewage, failing infrastructure

- **Transformation:** Rebirth, new attitudes and behaviors
  - *Renewal:* Revitalization, renovations, adaptive re-use

- **Apotheosis:** Final death and rebirth, ultimate reward
  - *Public Space:* Community, participatory politics, ritual

- **Return:** Mastery of both worlds, freedom to live, reconciliation of opposites
  - *A Foundation of Nature:* Inclusion, empathy, unity of urban/natural systems

There are a number of ways a city must be like a good story, in order to succeed. Not unlike Campbell's elements of a mythological story, the screenwriter Andrew Stanton, in a wonderful TED Talk, gives a number of guidelines for developing a memorable story.

- A story must promise us it will tell us a truth that deepens our understanding of who we are as human beings.

- Stories allow us to understand differences and similarities between ourselves and others.

- The greatest commandment of storytelling is "make me care."

- A story must make and keep a promise, that it will lead to something that is worth your time.

- Storytelling without dialogue is the purest form. The audience wants to work for its reward and participate in the story.

- A story must invoke wonder.

Cities would do well to emulate these guidelines.

Who are you? This simple line, delivered in a scene in the movie *Lawrence of Arabia* and is essential to any story It is powerful enough to have inspired Stanton in his own writing for such hit movies as *Finding Nemo* and *Toy Story*. A city will pose this question to us as well, when we think of it as a story in which we are immersed.

A successful city holds possibilities for each of us to create a personal story and to tell us its story in which we participate as actors. In this process we seek to learn who we are. But we'll never know what the endings will be.

Dreaming and Waking in the Streets of Paris

The Paris that the world has fallen so deeply in love with did not exist until about the early 1870's. Prior to that, the city had remained largely unchanged in its form for hundreds of years; an overcrowded medieval mess of narrow crooked streets lined with buildings sagging with age. There were certainly grand spaces – the Louvre and Tuileries – but the city as a whole was a cramped maze and impossible to traverse. The lack of water and sewer facilities gave rise to filth and regular outbreaks of disease.

Emperor Napoleon III appointed Eugene Baron Hausmann to oversee a massive renovation of the city of Paris, with few if any restrictions. From 1853 until 1870, Hausmann oversaw the construction of an extensive water and sewer system, numerous parks and civic buildings; and most notably, the demolition and renovation of multiple neighborhoods throughout the city. Today we recognize this work most easily in the many boulevards and avenues, boasting grand vistas and lined by elegant architecture and sidewalk cafes. Parisians of the time were grateful for the renewal and delighted by the elegance of the new spaces, though as is always the case, frustrated by the massive dislocation and high-handed dictatorial manner with which Hausmann operated. In the end, he built far more housing than he demolished, and gifted the city with an immediate improvement in public health. By 1870 however, citizens had had enough, and he was forced to resign. The legacy he left is a city universally considered one of the most beautiful in the world. Having lived in Paris several years as a small child, and visiting again numerous times as an adult, I have been shaped, emotionally and urbanistically, by the juxtaposition of these two worlds; the ancient and earthy medieval warrens lying between the elegant and airy cosmopolitan boulevards.

As to what Hausmann was able to accomplish, I'm intrigued by the thought of the psychological impact of the two experiences- walking the classic boulevard of grand vista and the ancient closed medieval passages. In terms of mythic symbolism of the psyche, I consider the straight, formal, and cosmopolitan boulevards of Hausmann as representing our rational consciousness; the ragged disjointed medieval passages as representing the irrational, unconscious dream state. In the interstices between the boulevards, the ancient crooked passageways still exist. One wanders semi-lost among the bent little alleys and then unexpectedly crosses onto a grand sunlit boulevard; it is much like awakening from a dream-state. Turn a corner and then dive back into the dream, in and out of consciousness, alleyway to avenue and back. The street, whether bright avenue or murky alley, is a thread, the warp and woof woven together into our life fabric.

As a species having evolved over multiple millions of years from unconscious instinct to conscious self-awareness, such an experience for us is a microcosm of the human movement toward the light. This movement toward the rational light gives us greater appreciation for both the conscious and unconscious aspects of our lives; by distinguishing one from the other, we can more clearly discover the value of each. But our foundation will always be that irrational, unconscious dream from which we emerged, deeply rooted and not to be ignored.

We are each of us a city, packed with residents making up various aspects of our personalities and inner psychic lives. We are never truly alone; we travel with our inner demons and angels. The entity we each think of as "me" is truly made up of characters and characteristics so independent of our control that we can think of ourselves as inhabited by a multitude of other beings. Today we tend to name these as various psychological traits and emotional conditions; our ancient ancestors named them as gods. One way to manage and interact with them is to personify them. When finding myself becoming angry, I might imagine meeting a character on a street in my 'city;' "oh, here is Mr. Jones again. Hello, listen, I don't have much time to spend with you at the moment, but I'll listen to what you have to say for a bit, so thanks for stopping by, good day." And with that acknowledgement of a fellow resident of my interior community, I dispense with my interaction with angry resentment. Or joy comes to us… "How delightful to see you Ms. Smith! Please join me and tell me your story as we walk." And so, we interact and learn from the many sides of ourselves which we may not know well enough or even acknowledge.

Bridges: Infrastructure and Relationship

At least twice a week I find myself riding the bicycle path along the Potomac River, from Arlington VA south to Old Town Alexandria or into downtown Washington. It's an excellent ride, with wide vistas, closed in woods, watery marshes, and views of the great American monuments—the Washington Monument, Lincoln and Jefferson Memorials— across the scenic river. The experience inspires me, calms me, excites me.

So, my frustration can be understood when one day I was greeted with an enormous gash in the greenery. A wooden fence had been erected around a construction site right on the river. Argh! What the hell was the Park Service/ Corps of Engineers/ Department of Something or Other, up to?! There was no one on site to ask. *Raggle fraggle snaggin #*&!&%#@* !!!* For a couple of weeks I swore and raged at this affront to nature.

Oh, of course. Finally a small sign was erected, giving an explanation: staging and construction zone for the repair of Memorial Bridge.

Like so much of America's infrastructure, Memorial Bridge was falling apart, badly. Carrying 68,000 vehicles per day, the bridge is undergoing three years of repair work at a price tag of $227 million. This should extend the life of the bridge by a good 85 years. I've heard that most of the world economy has less to do with innovation and creation of the new, and much more to do with repairing and maintaining what we already have. As a former landlord, I know that maintenance of the old can be much more expensive than construction of the new.

This isn't just any bridge across a river though; it is a metaphor of our national history. As early as the Andrew Jackson administration, a grand bridge was envisioned to symbolically unite the northern and southern states. No specific location or design was determined until the bridge as we know it was proposed in 1886. Designed by the famed McKim Mead & White, its construction was not complete until 1932. The location, set in the years after the Civil War, is unusual. Bridges are normally placed and aligned so as to increase commercial activity. Not so Memorial Bridge; the alignment does not connect two vital economic cores, but instead by either accident or intention, has a mission of telling a story. This can be easily seen in the two terminated vistas at either end; the Lincoln Memorial at one, Robert E. Lee's plantation home (Arlington House) and the National Cemetery at the other. The bridge acts as a visual reminder of the unity of the nation, the rift that occurred, and the desire to restore, and maintain, wholeness.

Of course, bridges only fulfill their objective if both sides are open and receptive. Around the turn of the last century and into the 1920's, our grandparents and great grandparents gifted us with invaluable infrastructure in the form of transportation networks, bridges, water and sewer systems. They did not, unfortunately, take into account the ongoing costs of maintenance. All at once and everywhere, as a result, we find that all these systems are crumbling at the same time. To add to the dilemma, our sense of national unity is crumbling as well… we find that not everyone wants connecting bridges, metaphorical or otherwise. The longer we wait to repair the damage, be it political, physical, or interpersonal the harder and more expensive it gets. Regular small maintenance projects and occasional large renovations are needed to avoid the loss of connection.

Most of the lessons of life have to do with relationship; how to make them work, how to keep them healthy, strong, and positive. Perhaps the construction and maintenance of bridges is a good metaphor for the basic work of our lives. We are, each of us, little neighborhoods so to speak, part of a larger whole, separated by rivers of misunderstanding. As a transportation corridor, a river acts to connect two distant points. By its very nature though, it also divides; it all depends on where you want to go. The next time you cross a bridge, remind yourself the importance of maintaining strong and respectful connections with others, especially those unlike yourself. The political and cultural divide we find ourselves in these days is affecting us as a nation but in our personal relationships. We need to put enormous effort into the repair and maintenance of our connecting fabric, both public as infrastructure and personal relationships. Get to work repairing those bridges, everyone.

Sewers and the Jungian Shadow

The Shadow, in psycho-spiritual terms developed by Carl Jung, represents aspects of ourselves that we have rejected and repressed, for any number of reasons, as being undesirable or negative. These aspects are not always negative, dark, or "evil" but are at odds with how we wish to see ourselves, or how we wish to be understood by the world. They arise out of experiences, often during childhood, which have caused emotional pain. We suppress these memories in order to avoid pain; the unintended consequence is it also blocks the process of psychological growth. We all possess a shadow side; it is a natural aspect of our spiritual psyche, but good emotional and spiritual health requires that we become aware of, accept, and integrate our shadow nature into our conscious awareness.

Beyond the individual shadow, there also seems to exist a collective Shadow, inherent in all humanity. This is easy enough to see in the daily news and history books.

Urban life too has its shadow aspects; elements which are inherent to civilization but too ugly for everyday viewing, so to speak. Trash, garbage, and sewage are by analogy the physical shadow of contemporary urban life. I suppose any land use rejected by the public, in "NIMBY" *(Not In My Back Yard)* fashion, might be considered such; industrial uses, trucking and warehousing, low-income housing, drug rehab centers… the general attitude is, "out of sight, out of mind." Toss out the garbage or flush the toilet, and be done. Yet all this waste doesn't disappear; it goes somewhere and has to be dealt with. Landfills and sewage treatment plants take care of this for us, because it simply has to be managed. The volume and toxicity of the refuse and waste we moderns produce is astonishing, but until recently we haven't really felt the need to think about it.

Coming to terms with one's shadow is typically part of a personal spiritual awakening or a psychological shift, often forced on a person by stressful circumstance. We need to do the same for our cities. Our infrastructure is crumbling from decades of neglect, and the environment is certainly going through unprecedented stresses; but our collective response is beginning to look encouraging.

Like an individual seeking to explore and integrate their shadow side, communities are beginning to bring their "dark side" into view, and find ways to turn problems into opportunities. The move toward "daylighting" is perhaps the most obvious and encouraging example. The term daylighting refers to the repair of former natural streams running through an urban area. As development took place early in the life a city or town, very often natural streams were channeled into underground pipes as part of the municipal stormwater system; streets would often be built on top of the former stream or creek. Daylighting uncovers these buried waterways, turning them back into natural corridors, bringing green open space, as parkland and wildlife habitat, back into the urban setting.

Stormwater has conventionally been seen as a nuisance, a problem to be dispatched as efficiently as possible. Out of the parking lot, off the street, into the sewer pipe, and done! Yet the long-term negative effect is at least two-fold. The first is to eliminate aquifer recharge, lowering the groundwater table. The second problem of treating rainwater as a problem requiring an engineered solution is that of pollution, particularly in older cities. Often, historic communities have combined sewer systems; both rainwater and sewage are conveyed in the same pipe. This might not be too bad during normal rain events, but heavier storms overload the system, requiring the treatment plant to be bypassed; raw sewage is then dumped directly into streams and rivers. As a method of easing the pressure on such combined systems, stormwater management policies now seek to allow rainwater to soak back into the ground, or be detained so that it can be slowly released and not overwhelm the system.

The move toward a more sustainable approach to the messier aspects of modern life is reflective of spiritual healing. Any issue, be it psychological in nature or the management of community infrastructure, is best served when we acknowledge its existence, bring it out in the open, and to turn what was once viewed as a problem into an opportunity. A spiritual journey is not always joy and light; we have to dig deep and uncover a lot of crap to find spiritual gems.

Weather, Seasons, and the Time of Day

Any place you choose to observe will never be the same twice. Small changes and shifts take place all the time, which can be hard to notice without focused attention. In an urban setting human activity is of course constantly re-working a place; but natural rhythms and cycles can sometimes be overlooked.

The angle of the sun and fullness of the moon each bring distinct patterns of light and shadow. Snow, rain, and dry heat each give to a place a completely different sensibility. Autumn leaves rattling, bare branches whistling with the wind, spring blossoms waving an invitation; morning, noon, and the lengthening shadows of afternoon, each reveal a different trait in the personality of a city.

How do people make use of space at different times under different conditions? Dupont Circle in DC is known locally as the place to be when snow falls, for the grand public snowball fight which always seem to spontaneously erupt on its own. From morning to evening, streets will experience commuters on foot, bike, and car all reversing their directions, like the twice-daily tides of the ocean. Quiet parks will see their energy level swell around lunchtime as office workers take an outdoor lunch break. All these, as we know, can affect, and reflect, our various moods and emotions, providing opportunity for observation and reflection.

Our thinking of the cycles of the day tends to focus, naturally enough, when we are awake. But what is there to discover, of self and city, in the deepest night? What goes on in a place when no one is there, in the small hours? What insights, spiritual and urbanistic, can be revealed to us when everyone else is asleep? I was inspired a couple of summers ago, as a result of enduring a very long walk home after a late-night social event, to make an intentional adventure; to choose locations that intrigue me, and experience them at a time when no one else would think to, say between the hours of 3:00 and 4:00 am. I wanted to see whether, as the poet Rupert Brooke tells us, *"Cities, like cats, will reveal themselves at night."*

Dyke Marsh and Crystal City

For several reasons, I chose to begin these adventures not in the city of Washington itself, but a park just outside the Beltway, along the Potomac River in Virginia. For a full urban experience, the whole of a region should be involved, not just downtown. So, a little bit of preserved nature set the tone. The location is also near the first boundary stone which gave Washington DC its shape, which seemed apt as a beginning point. Finally, my Tree is located there. I have formed a pretty close connection with one particular Linden tree; I read, write, and meditate under its branches, and it acts as a calming and centering influence, a doorway for my spiritual explorations, so to speak.

And what better time to begin of course, than under a full moon.

The full moon of July is known as the Hungry Ghost Moon in the Chinese tradition. I consider us all hungry ghosts in our essence, spirits temporarily embodied as human. When the hunger to grow and experience becomes overwhelming, we become incarnate, and like vampires, seek out what we need to feed, grow, and experience.

Vampires did appear that night in a sense, in the form of mosquitoes. More than I could bear... so much for meditating quietly with my Tree to ask Spirit for support and insight. Other than their buzzing though, what became apparent quickly was silence. At 2:30 am, the usual sounds of traffic along the George Washington Parkway, playing children, even the quacking of ducks, had stilled. The only activity I found came from unexpected encounters with wildlife. I had a staring contest with a beautiful red fox, and a race on my bike with a startled baby rabbit. I lost both times.

The start of this nocturnal roaming was a good 8 miles from home, and I was on my bike. To get away from the buzzing vampires and eventually get home, I decided to continue the night by riding back along Route 1, from Alexandria to Arlington. This took me through Crystal City and past the Pentagon. I quickly remembered that even at this time of night, 3 am, even very light traffic on suburban streets is far more frightening than on more urban ones. Suburbia as a design model is completely focused on cars, and averse to anything unusual or unexpected, such as a bicyclist.

Crystal City is an essentially linear corridor of 1960's-era office towers running parallel to the Potomac River near National Airport. It has been trying to reposition itself as something more than a soul-less office canyon, and is slowly perking up with residential and entertainment uses. For the most part though it still feels strained; street– level commercial activity in what felt like every third building consists of enormous gym clubs, each displaying three dozen stationary bike machines. I noted the irony and rode on.

In various urban parks, Arlington County has seen fit to begin placing wooden bars across the seats of park benches, to discourage the homeless from sleeping rough in public spaces. Perhaps this was the cause of the homeless camp I stumbled upon in a side corner of parking lot at Target. So many of our municipal management and land use decisions end up not really solving a problem so much as merely shifting it elsewhere. Not unlike much of our psychic lives I suppose; putting a patch over a problem doesn't make it go away; it just pops up again elsewhere in some other form. Perhaps homelessness should be thought of not as a problem in itself, but a symptom of some larger failing.

Aside from mosquitoes and some homeless brethren, the most common sign of life at 3 am comes in the form of maintenance workers. The late-night silence was broken only by my pedaling, until a jackhammer shook me out of the calm. Sewer and street repairs have to take place sometime, and a crew of workmen were hard at the task of repairing a broken pipe. We rely so much on this hidden infrastructure and rarely give it a moments consideration. So too are our lives reliant on our unconscious, the unseen, foundational infrastructure of our lives. Aren't our dreams like those workmen, appearing at night to repair and maintain our psychic being?

14th Street, Shaw, and Blagden Alley

While the evocative sensual experience of the first late-night adventure was silence, on this occasion it was the cool temperature and soft breeze. It's definitely *not* what is expected of an August night in Washington DC. On a bike at 3 am in shorts and T-shirt, it was almost too cool. It helped wake me up though, and somehow gave a sense of timelessness to the night.

The quiet, deserted hour of 3:00 in the morning is still much more active than expected, with quite a few bikes on the street, mostly restaurant workers heading home. Even a pedicab was still cruising for paying passengers, with more hope than success. The lights inside the iconic Bens Chili Bowl revealed a few people still hungry enough to risk heartburn.

Away from the shuttered bars and restaurants of 14th and U Streets, on 9th, things calmed down even more. Traffic was thin enough so that I felt like I owned the streets, riding down the center without a care. The homeless and late-night locals want to know what I was up to… if I'm not out to score drugs, what the hell am I doing here now?! One tries to give me the usual patter, his practiced line about needing money since by the grace of God he just arrived from Carolina. He figures me out quickly enough to drop that and we chat about life a bit before moving on. Turning up an alley, I veer to avoid a couple of what I thought were old paint cans, only to discover they were the booted feet of a homeless man sleeping in a doorway.

The alleys of the Shaw neighborhood no longer have the amount of trash or graffiti I remember from my semi-punk days in the 1980's, but still enough to make it clear that it isn't completely gentrified, still has something of a scrappy edge. Completely different worlds can occupy the same space for very different purposes. The juxtaposition of hipster renovations and the long-time working class give a sense of adjacent secret intimacies, with neither culture truly knowing the other, yet influencing each other in ways they may not even recognize.

Blagden Alley and the adjacent Naylor Court strike me as excellent examples of this. The near-downtown neighborhoods of DC were at one time crisscrossed with service alleys, home to horse stables, warehouses, workshops, and barely-habitable housing for the underclass. Those that remain today went through a long period of decline, eventually dissolving into almost complete abandonment. For about the past twenty years though, Blagden Alley been the home of upscale restaurants and residences, craft cocktail lounges, coffee bars, and creative class consulting outfits. Perhaps its defining feature is the public artwork adorning various walls and garage doors. To really get a feel of what the place has been over time requires a late-night visit, when the current life does not dominate, and the energy of history can be more easily felt. Blagden Alley lies at the confluence of three worlds; the downtown professional crowd, uptown creatives, and long-time working-class African Americans. These edges where various cultural ecosystems meet, are much like natural points of transition; ocean and beach, field and forest, jungle and savannah, day and night. It is at such places that different species, and different cultures, intermingle and make unexpected magic happen.

Whatever insights can be found on deserted night-time streets are visible to us during daylight hours, but there are other things to focus on then, blocking any ability to take it all in. Spending time on the streets at the late hours before dawn is a bit of a waking dream; the unconscious of the city rises more easily to awareness. A city is all about the gathering of people, but really making sense of both the place and its inhabitants, for me, comes by observing a place not only with them, but also in their absence; the ancestors speak more clearly then.

Questions to Ponder

- What psychic meaning do I project onto various physical and social aspects of my city?

- Which neighborhoods represent specific characteristics I find within myself?

- Do I think of myself in terms of a character in a story depending on where I find myself?

CHAPTER V

The Alchemists

"That which we need most will be found where we least want to go" —Carl Jung

The Alchemical Wedding; by Philippa Shanks

YOU ARE A CITY

A SMALL, OBSCURE, AND LARGELY FORGOTTEN CORNER OF OUR cultural heritage remains a surprisingly valuable resource for psychic exploration and growth, and yes, even for renewing our relationship to the city; that is, alchemy. Reaching back at least to ancient Egypt in its earliest foundations, it held a place of high regard for thousands of years, until its slow demise with the rise of the Enlightenment and the rational scientific method. Indeed, Isaac Newton, a familiar and foundational name in the development of early scientific inquiry, is considered to be one of the last of the true alchemists. Entire libraries have been devoted to the subject of alchemy, and its heritage in the worlds of ancient Egypt, Greece, medieval Europe, Arabia, and China. I cannot hope to add anything to such a deeply complex and ornate subject. Yet I will contend that any attempt to consider urbanism from a spiritually curious perspective can gain something positive and useful from it.

The current popular use of the term "alchemy" seems to imply a sort of serendipity. I often see the term used to describe a rather free-form activity or experience of synchronicity - yet another misunderstood term. Something is thought of as "alchemical" if there is an element of unplanned spontaneity resulting in a positive yet unexpected solution; one plus one equals three, so to speak. Yet true spiritual alchemy was very much a work of process and procedure, and largely metaphorical. Our image of alchemy is of an odd combination of mysticism and chemistry; of wizard-like characters in dark basements surrounded by chemicals, fires, boiling liquids in glass beakers, and other bits of laboratory equipment. Although the practical side of alchemy had always involved itself in such fields as medicine, metallurgy, and military explosives, for our purposes the psychological element takes precedence here. Far from the conventional image of alchemy as an amateurish attempt to turn lead into gold, or even an early attempt at developing the scientific method, alchemy had at its core a spiritual discipline.

The cliché of trying to turn lead into gold speaks to a psychological metaphor, not simply a chemistry experiment. What was being attempted was first to gain an understanding of the mind of God by discovering the workings of the physical world, and thus also bring to a leaden human life the golden light of spiritual wisdom. Each alchemist seemed to have developed their own symbolic and metaphorical language to describe the process, making it all incredibly obscure, but there were normally four to seven stages of transformation, centered on the dissolution and re-integration of various aspects of the soul or psyche, as represented by chemical processes.

Alchemy truly seems like an obscure and long outdated rabbit-hole to dive into. However, by the end of this chapter, I hope to reveal how an understanding of its methods and processes can benefit one's personal spiritual practice, and create an approach to viewing our urban settings as alchemical laboratories of soul work.

A Brief History of Alchemy

Many scholars will point to ancient Egypt as the earliest foundation of the tradition of alchemy. Specifically, the Egyptian practice of mummification was the source. This seems to make sense, when considering that mummification was a process of physically preserving the body as a spiritual home for the soul. Getting the materials and chemicals just right was crucial; the process was all about physical transformation in support of spiritual transformation.

A second and more ancient source for the magical process of physical transformation is found in mining, metallurgy, and blacksmithing. For most if not all of our pre-history, all of nature was understood to be alive, including simple rock and stone. The earliest metal workers thus viewed ores and minerals to be living entities, buried in the womb of mother earth. Their practice of mining, metallurgy, and smithing was for them a sort of obstetric operation, aiding in the birth, development, and transmutation of these "children." This of course required special rituals to obtain permission for such an invasive process. What could possibly more alchemical than the process of mining a raw metal, heating and purifying it, and shaping it, bringing it to maturation, so to speak?!

Alchemy as we imagine it today came to Europe much later, in a roundabout fashion. The Arab world initially picked up the process of this earth-based spiritual inquiry from Egypt, from whom the Greeks later learned. They in turn passed on the knowledge and practice to Europe, particularly through the writings of Zosimos, roughly in the year 300.

A strong but independent heritage of alchemy is also to be found in ancient India and China. Very few women were involved; perhaps fifteen are known to us now; notable individuals being Maria Prophetissa, Cleopatra (no, not *that* one), both of whom were contemporaries of Zosimos, and on to Isabella Cortese and Catarina Sforza in Renaissance Italy. Even Queen Elizabeth I of England had a strong interest in the work.

The practice of alchemy was widely known in Europe for hundreds of years but hit its high mark in the 1500's and early 1600's, just prior to its decline. Even so, its practitioners tended to be secretive, due to active harassment from the Catholic Church. Its slow demise began in the mid 1600's with the Enlightenment, the rise of rationalism and the scientific method, and the accompanying decline of spiritual sensibilities. At this time, alchemists increasingly emphasized the emerging practice of scientific chemistry rather than seeking psychic insight into the nature of God's world. Surprisingly though, according to Carl Jung, this was the point at which a few alchemists began to more consciously emphasize the fundamentally personal nature of their work. Particularly in the writings of Jacob Boehme, Gerhard Dorn, and Michael Maier in the early 1600's was such an understanding made explicit; that what was involved was an inquiry into the personal spiritual life of the practitioner, not only a generalized search for the spiritual meaning of the physical world. While others preceding them had such a sense, the grounding had always been, at least consciously, an exploration of the spiritual foundations of the physical world, of matter; in other words, gaining an understanding of the physical world and its substances could bring insight into God's intentions. The unconscious intention was another matter.

Their (mostly) Unconscious Methods

Carl Jung was an early scholar of alchemy, writing and researching on the subject for over 30 years. With the perspective he cultivated, and as a psychologist, he discerned that the medieval alchemists were perhaps a bit at odds with themselves, involved in two separate lines of inquiry, one conscious and one unconscious. The conscious and intentional line focused on an attempt to understand God through the workings of the fundamental elements of nature. How does God work, and why? Perhaps this can be revealed by understanding the processes of nature, they conjectured. The heating, combining, and otherwise manipulating of various chemicals was primary, with sulfur, salt, and mercury playing prominent roles. Such processes and materials held symbolic meaning. Sulfur, for instance, represented dryness, heat, and masculinity. Mercury, given its physical characteristic of seeming both solid and liquid, was considered a transformational element reaching beyond heaven and earth. Alchemists would carefully observe the results of their operations, seeking to find symbolic meaning in order to discern God's intentions for creation. This process of observation was done with great spiritual intention, in a prayerful manner requiring the practitioner to take on rites of purification. In all this, they opened themselves up to mystical visions.

The second, unconscious inquiry was focused on the practitioners' individual soul, or psyche as we might phrase it today. As an alchemist developed a relationship to his psyche, or soul, during his procedures, the soul gained an opening to communicate what it wanted to reveal and make conscious about the alchemist himself, not necessarily about God and his physical world.

The tools used in alchemical work, along with the materials and processes, need some explanation. Essentially the process of alchemy is that of transforming a variety chemicals and metals, breaking them apart and re-combining them. Heating, cooling, moistening and drying, condensing, combining and separating, and burning were all a part of this process. The elements being manipulated included sulfur, salt, mercury, and various others. This took place with a variety of specialized tools; glass alembics, beakers, and retorts, iron and clay pots, and furnaces. Fire was essential, and was treated as both a tool and element.

Obscure language and odd metaphors were the stock in trade for the alchemist and their "recipes." There were two reasons for this; first, to protect the alchemist from harassment from the Catholic Church; and also, to protect their efforts from unscrupulous charlatans. Innumerable "recipes" were developed, which are to this day difficult to interpret. A passage from one work, The Book of Lambspring, serves as an example:

The Sages will tell you that two fishes are in our sea without any flesh or bones.

Let them be cooked in their own water; then they also will become a vast sea, the vastness of which no man can describe.

Moreover, the Sages say that the two fishes are only one, not two; they are two, and nevertheless they are one, Body, Spirit, and Soul.

Now, I tell you most truly, cook these three together, that there may be a very large sea. Cook the sulphur well with the sulphur,

And hold your tongue about it: conceal your knowledge to your own advantage, and you shall be free from poverty. Only let your discovery remain a close secret.

My sense is that a third reason for such convoluted language can be seen in the fact that so much of the work of the alchemist was an unconscious communication between the conscious ego of the alchemist and their unconscious psyche. The psyche does not speak our language and must use metaphor. The well-known psychological process of unconscious projection takes place in this. The alchemists projected meaning into both the processes and elements they worked with. Thus the florid imagery in alchemical writings.

The effort to achieve a "union of opposites" was fundamental to the process, often referred to as the "chymical wedding." Good and evil, day and night, hot and cold, male and female, wet and dry, and so on. Images and references to the

King and Queen thus figure prominently. This union of opposites also plays a significant role in Jung's psychological process, as we can detect in his concept of individuation or psychic development.

Jung and His Alchemical Psychology

There are innumerable approaches, in history and around the globe, to spiritual and psychological development and enlightenment. Here we are focused on alchemy, and the best way I know to make any sense of it is through the work of Carl Jung. He was able to clarify and organize the meaning of the intentionally confused language of the alchemists, and give it its proper place within the global tradition of spiritual quest.

The first inkling Jung had that alchemy could be a source of psychological insight came, not surprisingly, in the form of a dream. In this dream, Jung saw himself in a library filled with books from the 1500's and 1600's, which contained odd symbols and characters. Initially dismissing alchemy as just so much silly foolishness, he nonetheless began collecting such alchemical texts as he recalled from his dream, but could not make any sense of them for many years. In 1929 he was asked to write the introduction to *The Secret of the Golden Flower*, a treatise on the ancient Chinese heritage of Taoist alchemy. At this time, he was working on a comparative analysis of psycho/ spiritual traditions, and the insight then came to him, that alchemical processes were equivalent to the steps he was developing for his own methods of psychotherapy.

As distinct from other approaches to psychotherapy, Jung's intentions do not focus on bringing comfort and release from neurosis by teaching how to manage emotions and relationships, and fit into social norms more cleanly. Rather, Jung's intention was to bring one into relationship with the "numinous;" the soul or the psychic unconscious, so that one rises above normative society. The issue causing a neurosis does not disappear so much as become irrelevant; that is to say, our problems do not diminish but we grow larger and more expansive, with greater capacity and understanding in our widened horizons. Life may remain just as difficult but we are to gain greater perspective, making what was previously troublesome less so. The intention is to develop a life of meaning and purpose through connection to the larger Self, not mere happiness.

Another more succinct way of phrasing this, the source of which I cannot find, is the following: "After each stage of ego death, the new ego that emerges is less brittle, more resilient. What might destroy a person in their sixth level of growth, the first iteration could not have survived the mere contemplation of." The process of psychological growth results in fewer and fewer things in life being large enough to disturb us.

Jung viewed the process of alchemy as a high point of spiritual development for the western world, and at least procedurally, the equivalent of his process of psychological development, known as individuation. Marie-Louise von Franz, one of Jung's greatest students and collaborators, put all this in a more contemporary psychological phrasing for us: "As physics is a mental reconstruction of material processes, perhaps a physical reconstruction of psychic processes is possible in nature itself." This implies to my mind the possibility of making use of the city through a process of symbolic understanding. More on this below.

The structure of the psyche, as Jung understood it, contains the ability to dissolve itself, in a manner of speaking, and then re-assemble itself with a more integrated and developed system. This allows for newly revealed aspects of the psyche to be developed and integrated. This is indeed how we grow and mature psychologically, in an alchemical process; the breaking apart and re-assembling of various aspects of our personality, both conscious and unconscious, purified and strengthened. Below is an outline of this process.

The Stages of Alchemical Psychic Transformation

To make clear once again, alchemy was, for centuries, an attempt to understand the relationship between the physical and spiritual realms, and God's intentions, by gaining an understanding of the physical world and how it operates. The physical world, it was understood, is a mere reflection of the spiritual; "as above, so below" as it was phrased. But to the extent that the spiritual world resides within us, alchemy essentially evolved a process of self-reflection, for the purpose of psychic growth and spiritual enlightenment, in spite of the fact that its practitioners were not always aware precisely what they were up to.

Alchemy was very much a study in process. Sometimes four, or seven, and even as many as fifteen separate steps, or "operations," are taken in an alchemical process of psychic development; from the breaking apart of old values, habits, and beliefs to identify the parts, through transformation of those parts, and on to the union of these renewed components. Jung himself identified four steps in his alchemically based psychology. These are as follows:

1. **Nigredo (the Blackening):** What we now term shadow work, confession, and catharsis. This involves understanding archetypes and their dynamics, discovering and managing one's personal complexes and projections.

2. **Albedo (the Whitening):** The process of illumination and elucidation. This is the development of communication between the conscious ego and the unconscious (anima or animus). Dreams, interpreting symbols, and active imagination are tools used here.

3. **Citrinitas (the Yellowing):** A stage of education. Here we discover how to develop more conscious relationships with the various aspects of our unconscious, and thus with other individuals.

4. **Rubedo (the Reddening):** The process of developing an authentic personal myth and symbolic life, the true persona; and the formation of more highly developed relationships with other individuals and the wider world.

As mentioned above, each alchemist tended to develop their own processes, symbols, and even terminology. While Jung made use of the four steps outlined above, another common approach involved seven stages:

1. **Calcination:** Chemically, this involved heating a substance over a flame, burning it down to ashes. Psychologically, this represents the breaking down of ego and attachment.

2. **Dissolution:** This involved dissolving the ashes in water. This represents the drop into an exploration of the unconscious, which water represents. This brings out hidden aspects of ourselves of which we were not aware.

3. **Separation:** This step involved the isolation and filtering of the elements that have been dissolved. This stage of self-development is a review of the psychic elements that have been revealed, and a consideration of what can be made use of and integrated. This, along with step 2, are commonly known as shadow work.

4. **Conjunction:** A new substance is created from the remaining selected elements. This is the psychological effort to bring together the conscious and unconscious; all the dualities that our found within us are to be integrated into a new vision of the self.

5. **Fermentation:** The substance that has been produced is then broken down or allowed to rot, in order to test its strength. This is a testing of the new material; does our new psychic insight have the strength to survive suffering and adversity?

6. **Distillation:** The solution or material is boiled and condensed to increase purity. At this stage, we test the ego to ensure it no longer controls our assumptions and mode of being.

7. **Coagulation:** The material being worked with transforms into a solid. This is psychologically equivalent to the union of opposites, the full integration of dualities, in which we live with a full merging of the physical and spiritual. It is equivalent to reaching Nirvana, or as the alchemists termed it, finding the Philosopher's Stone.

Whether we consider alchemy as process of four steps or seven, certain basic aspects are involved. These include the breaking apart of a whole, examining the parts, transforming those parts, and re-assembling the parts back into a newly formed and integrated whole. For myself, I find the following language easier to understand and work with:

- Examine the various aspects of my conscious ego personality;

- Break apart the barrier between my conscious ego and the larger unconscious self;

- Examine and learn to relate to what is found in the unconscious. This involves two stages, a. shadow work or the full acceptance of one's darkest side, and b. develop relationship to and conversation with the anima/ animus (the soul);

- Bring what is found in the unconscious forward, into conscious everyday life – then relate, with body, mind, and soul, with other individuals and the wider world of shared culture.

A study of alchemy gives us more than historical context of ourselves. It provides an understanding of the archetypes of change. Jung saw that the psyche has the ability to "dissolve" in order to re-construct itself in a more whole and balanced form. The phases of alchemy and the associated archetypes can bestow upon us a larger perspective, giving a deeper understanding of the phases of our life and its purpose.

Clearly, we do not transform the soul all at once; or rather, building a connection to soul does not transform us all at once. Relationship with the soul is the way we develop and strengthen the conscious ego. A more conscious ego in turn is the tool that the unconscious uses to learn. The two sides teach each other in mutual conversation.

And finally, the big question remains; how does all this relate to the city? Where does the experience of place fit into this process of alchemical psychic development? Isn't the city the last place we would imagine for all this to take place, with all its worldly distractions, the dirt and noise and ignorant unruly crowds?

An Urban Alchemy for Today

The world of ancient and medieval practitioners of alchemy had no connection to urban planning or design, or really the life of the community as a whole.

Alchemy has always been a very private and introspective effort. There is however one aspect of alchemy which is pertinent to our consideration of urban settings. That is an almost completely unknown and astonishing assumption of the alchemical heritage, shared alike by the medieval European, Chinese, and Arabic traditions. Not only was the human to be transformed and elevated, but the Divine must also be freed. The alchemists were certain that the physical world itself, not just we humans, was in need of redemption. In the alchemical tradition, God was within in nature, actually inside the physical elements, and asleep. God, like we his creatures, is need of release and awakening. Alchemy sought not simply the development and healing of the person; the Creator too was asleep inside physical matter and in need of awakening. Alchemy was a search for release of both the human soul and Divine matter. This harkens back to the ideas mentioned above, of early metallurgical mysticism conceiving of ores and minerals as infants in need of refinement. With this concept, we can see the idea of projection once again; is it God trapped in the material elements that must be awakened; or is it our souls seeking relationship with us yet trapped in our unconscious?

An understanding of the fundamental nature of the elements was therefore essential, as well as how these interact with one another. Is this not a clear metaphor for our modern understanding of our own psyche, made up as it is of archetypal images and energies? To understand ourselves we must understand the most fundamental elements of our nature, the totality of both the dark and light within ourselves. Gaining an understanding of one's conscious ego personality is just the beginning; discovering the darkness of one's shadow, the mystery of the anima or animus, both hidden in the unconscious, is the major work.

The alchemists would say that in order for the technical and physical side of alchemical transformation to work properly, the alchemist himself needs to be purified and transformed as well. The inquiry into God's physical world is holy work, so the alchemist must likewise be in a holy state. This conjures in my mind an image of our contemporary research scientists donning protective gowns and masks so as to mar their work, or be marred by it.

If the alchemists projected their psychic contents into various elements such as mercury, salt, and sulfur, searching for insight, what could an urbanist or city-dweller project into? Streets, alleys, parks, monuments, and so on; the various physical aspects of the built environment. In this way we make use of the archetypes of urbanism; the use of metaphor is to my mind a sort of "intentional" projection. Or rather, we might say that metaphor is a projection made conscious. By the act of experiencing a city or town with intention, to infuse our observations of urbanism with myth and metaphor and meaning, we liberate the city from mere physical infrastructure, assist in the birth of new purpose for both ourselves and our place.

We can learn to read the city as an enormous alchemical classroom filled with symbols, their meaning obscured unless we take the effort to decipher them.

The tools and elements of my urban laboratory are many: the ordinary street, the grand avenue, the dark and dirty alley. The green park, street lamps, fire hydrants, benches. The list is long; if we are open to the voice of our unconscious, these elements and others can be the language of its message. The soul is not fluent in English or any other human language, but makes use of the images in our world of experience. And not only the physical elements but the activities we observe and take part in. Waiting at that bus stop, celebrations in the plaza, meeting friends randomly on a sidewalk. Observe and reflect on all this … ask the soul what it makes of all this. Have a conversation together.

We won't be unconsciously projecting into chemicals the activity of our psyche, as the alchemists seem to have done. Instead, we will make use of a conscious understanding of archetypes of urbanism, coupled with what the unconscious wishes to teach us or ask of us. The surrounding city space provides not only the elements with which we work, but a vessel into which the unconscious can pour itself for our consideration. Can we say that metaphor is a projection made conscious? We can use the urban space surrounding us to create a vessel, a temenos, into which the unconscious can pour itself for our consideration.

For our purposes, the tools and the elements are almost one and the same. The tools *are* the elements, understood as archetypes. The elements themselves become metaphors. When we view physical elements of urbanism as archetypes, they transition to the role of the alchemical elements.

Imagine the setting of the city, with its streets, plazas, and buildings, as equivalent to an alchemical laboratory, outfitted with all the tools and equipment of the alchemist. This is our version of their glass jars and alembics, retorts, bowls, fire and water. This is available to us on a daily basis, ready for us to make use of in our own psychic experiments. The street as the path of my life, the intersection representing the decisions I must make. The dark and dirty back alleys are reminiscent of my more unsavory self, the sewer drains and hidden pipes providing a repository for my ugliest unwanted shadow. Is an office building reflective of my persona? That bus stop crowded with impatient commuters – are they not representative of the various characters making up the population of interior citizenry of my soul?

There is a small triangular park along Connecticut Avenue in Washington where I go several times each month, to sit quietly observing and reflecting on the ways in which the surrounding city mirrors my own interior life. Surrounded by a heavily trafficked avenue and two busy downtown streets, Longfellow Park is surprisingly calm amidst so much activity. It functions as lunchtime refuge for nearby office workers, a meeting place for casual conversations, a base camp for the community of downtown delivery drivers, a temporary haven for the homeless, a reading room for students. A bus stop ensures a constant flow of short-term inhabitants. Shrubbery, several crape myrtles, a slight elevation, and a couple of large basswood trees, my personal favorite, provide a sense of enclosure. The focal point of course is a statue of the namesake poet Henry Wadsworth Longfellow, seated with a book in his lap, contemplating the scene before him. Observation and reflection. All this in a space smaller than a typical suburban quarter acre residential lot.

Longfellow Park is a temenos, a sacred, bounded, and protected space of observation and reflection. A meditative space amidst the surrounding activity of the city. The energy of the place rises and falls, ebbs and flows throughout the day, the surrounding traffic flowing like blood through the city's veins. I scan the scene on all sides; people interacting with or avoiding one another; chattering, sauntering, or rushing maniacally. Then I sit with eyes closed, taking in only the sound all about me; birds in the trees, voices, scooters, horns honking like the geese flying overhead, doors banging, and the wind rustling the leaves above me. The interior noise of the overactive mind is somehow calmed by the exterior action of my surroundings. I am able to become an impartial outside observer of my own interior life, by transferring it out to the city around me and interacting with it.

Questions to Ponder

- What psychic meaning do I project onto various physical and social aspects of my city?

- Does the city go through alchemical transformation? How does that represent my own transformation?

- In what way is God "trapped and asleep" in the physical elements and processes of the city? Is this a way of understanding that the unconscious is trapped and asleep inside me as well?

CHAPTER VI

The Flaneur

―――――――――

*"Every path, every street in the world
is your walking meditation path."*—Thich Naht Hahn

17th and S Streets NW, Washington, D.C.

THE MOST FUNDAMENTAL WAY IN WHICH WE PARTICIPATE with any urban space, the most immediate and intimate experience of place, is by walking. Up until the 20th century, cities had always been designed with walking as the basic assumption. Well, of course, how else would you get around? The ability to walk to all one's daily needs for work, for food, to socialize, and everything else, was so obvious that it hardly needed mentioning, until the advent of cars. Automobiles made suburban living the default it is today; as a result, walking has become so difficult in many communities that it is sometimes made illegal for schoolchildren to walk to school. In response to this situation, many communities promote wooded walking trails as a recreational amenity. But beyond these two attitudes of walking, as recreation and as practical necessity, a third option is occasionally heard from; walking as spiritual exercise.

What a Flaneur Does

Dictionary.com defines the term Flaneur as an idler, dawdler, loafer. A very thin, shallow, and offensive definition; Merriam-Webster isn't any better. A playful term is a good alternative: Coddiwomple (v.) – To travel in a purposeful manner towards a vague destination. But I prefer my own definition: a passionate yet detached wandering observer of city life. The first use of the term is generally given to the French writer Baudelaire in about 1854. The habit however may have its origin with Louis Mercier, a writer and newspaper reporter more than 50 years earlier. He wrote about everything he saw, the everyday life of ordinary people on the streets, and ended up publishing 12 volumes of sketches.

Not a dilettante nor a dandy, who is cynical, detached, and intentionally creates scenes, a flaneur (or the feminine, flaneuse) is a calm observer, bearing witness to the lives of fellow urban dwellers. A flaneur is generally singular, isolated. The classic Parisian flaneur will definitely make eye contact with passers-by, but never smiles or gives greeting. It is a private meditative spirituality. Being naturally gregarious, I can't help but strike up brief conversations with strangers, perhaps crossing the line from private spirituality to the sociability of religion. Who knows what may come up in such brief conversation; personal stories, cooking advice, travel tips, humorous pet stories… random stories from people one might otherwise never meet. The city is usually considered to be a lonely place, but only if you're unwilling to take a few chances. Christopher Butler is said to have understood the flaneur as seeking a form of transcendence, to "find the eternal in the transitory." City life is almost universally said to have a negative impact on the human psyche, but what are the positives? The flaneur is out to find them. Without necessarily intending a meditative or prayerful effort, the flaneur is open to it merely by reducing oneself to the act of observing, of being present in the moment.

The intentionality of having no intentions allows the opportunity for the unexpected to break through. It is meditation in motion; observing and being fully present to the moment, letting it go, releasing the experience and being open to the next. The flaneur is giving a new twist to the perhaps overused term of the moment, "mindfulness," generally described as being present to and observant of one's own internal state of being – breath, heartbeat, emotional state. But can flaneury not be an equivalent effort at being present to one's external surroundings? The sounds and activity of the adjacent street, sidewalk, people… By simply observing, taking it all in and letting it all go, we can find our center no matter the setting.

The path a flaneur may take is one of personal preference, and might constantly change. Or not; one might choose one particular route, and stick with it, never deviating. Others may choose to never repeat the same route twice. A flaneur may choose to incorporate their practice into daily errands, walking to the pharmacy or corner grocery. Rules might be set: always take the third left turn, or turn right if you see a parent pushing a child in a stroller. Time might figure in: the flaneur might decide to walk their route only on Saturday mornings, or over the lunch hour during an office weekday. I often sit at a window seat at a favorite cafe in downtown Washington DC, and regularly observe one particular individual walking the same route at the same time, every day. Is she a flaneuse? Who knows, but she radiates a sense of calm reflection. At such times, sitting in that café observing the world go by, perhaps I am operating as a "stationary" flaneur.

Aside from that "stationary" practice, I have formed multiple routes for myself. One involves a short loop around my home neighborhood, another larger one of several blocks around Farragut Square in downtown Washington DC, and a very extensive half-day route around Dupont Circle. More on that in a later chapter.

Tai Chi and Meditative Walking

There is no telling how many of my fellow professional urban planners put much thought into the mere act of walking. Walkability and neighborhood walk scores, yes; but the physical act of walking really had not crossed my mind. For an urbanist, walkability and the experience of place is fundamental and is a real joy. For a spiritually curious individual, awareness of self and surroundings is just as essential if not more so. Now, I'm increasingly paying attention to how I walk. I've found that the simple act of walking down the street can be an opportunity for more than merely getting from one place to another; even more than pleasant entertainment. There are several different ways to do it I suppose, depending on your goals, and how busy the sidewalk is.

I try to be aware of both the act and experience of walking, using diverse sources of inspiration. On crowded, busy sidewalks, my practice of Tai Chi comes to mind. A few years ago, a mentor suggested I take up Tai Chi or Qi-Gong as part of my spiritual practice. Back in high school I took a few years of Shorin Ryu karate, so the idea made sense to me. I tried a Tai Chi session and it immediately resonated. I've been taking classes ever since.

If Tai Chi is at all on your radar, you likely get an image of a slow-motion exercise that groups of retirees practice in public parks. Far more than that, Tai

Chi is a foundational nexus between Taoist philosophy and martial arts. A basic concept of Taoism is Wu wei, which means non-action or non-doing; that is, acting in a natural, un-contrived way. The goal of spiritual practice is, according to Lao Tzu in his work, the Tao te Ching, the attainment of this purely natural way of behaving. Another way of thinking about Wu wei of "action that does not involve struggle or excessive effort." The concept of "effortless action" is foundational to Tai Chi. As a martial art, it assumes your opponent is larger, stronger, faster. Therefore, do not act as the aggressor, but allow your opponent's energy to work against him. Be fluid like water, it teaches; few movements are ever made directly, but rather obliquely. Walking against the flow of a crowded sidewalk is much the same. One cannot simply barge ahead; passers-by, trash cans, pets on leashes, and abandoned scooters have to be avoided. A rather good attitude for life in general; Tai Chi can be thought of as meditation in motion. As I walk a busy sidewalk on Connecticut Avenue in DC, or King Street in Alexandria, I find myself weaving in the side-to-side dodge of Tai Chi, avoiding the aggression of the oncoming flow, and focusing on the moment, the simple act of taking one step after another.

In calmer settings such as a neighborhood park or quiet residential street, a different source of insight inspires me. Walking comes as naturally to us as anything, but the Zen Buddhist teacher, Thich Nhat Hanh reveals in his small book, How to Walk, reveals that the simple act of walking is an opportunity for gratitude and joy. He taught "mindful walking" for seventy years, until his recent death. Meditation, he shows us, is not always sedentary. He imparts a number of practical tips, some basics which I share here. First, set for yourself a simple intention to enjoy and be aware of the basic process of walking. Focus solely on each step and breath. Make a contract between yourself and a particular place to practice mindful walking. Choose a particular stretch of road, or around a certain block, or while running a specific errand on foot. Finally, match your breathing with your pace. Perhaps begin with two steps as you inhale, three steps with each exhale. Adjust according to topography and your own comfort.

What makes a sidewalk, crowded or not, conducive to these sorts of meditative walking? Perhaps the closest that sidewalk design comes to promoting, or at least accommodating, meditative walking, is found in the art of walkable placemaking. Our experience of sidewalks is of course at a basic, personal level. The act of meditation is what we bring to the place. Sidewalk design can be a lot more complicated than we think! Although meditation is not a design criterion I'm aware of, there are lots of roles sidewalks have to play, and their design takes some subtle consideration. Just as the cartway of a street has distinct lanes, for travel, turning, and parking, so too do sidewalks, particularly in commercial areas. Physically, they have four layers: a frontage zone adjacent to buildings, which accommodates signage, displays, and maybe outdoor seating; a thoroughfare zone, for foot travel, wide enough for pedestrian comfort; a furnishing zone, for tree wells or planters, and furniture such as trash cans, benches, and the like; and an edge zone, a narrow bit wide enough to give space for people to get in and out of parked cars.

Sidewalks aren't designed with a layer designated for meditation, but they can provide plenty to meditate on, and pay attention to. Done gracefully, all of this adds up to a positive and immersive pedestrian environment, both pleasing and practical. Are mindfulness and walkability at odds here? While meditative walking is typically an inward-looking effort, a well-designed sidewalk, with good adjacent uses and window design, also offers the outward– looking meditative setting for that third sort of meditative walking discussed earlier, that of the flaneur. Sometimes a little space to breath—or walk—is all we need to start a new path.

How to Discover a New City

When I was 24 and could find no intentional plan or direction for my life, I decided to live in Brussels. Ostensibly, this was an agreement with my father to prepare for a career in the Foreign Service. Hang around the European Commission headquarters, hone my French language skills, make a few connections and prepare for a career as a diplomat. Instead, I volunteered with a Flemish non-profit construction company, learning the Dutch language and helping to build an orphanage and drug rehab center. I made the right choice.

Trying to get myself acclimated to a city divided into two unwilling halves (French-speaking Walloons, the Flemish with their Dutch language), I decided the best way to discover my way around was to intentionally get lost. I lived near the Jacques Brel Station in Anderlecht, so I took the metro to the far northeastern end of the line, in Stokkel, and walked back, to see what there was to see. Of course, it was a bit too much of an all- day and night hike, but it was a wonderful experience, with so much to discover. There was nothing in particular I wanted to see, I just wanted to be in the middle of something new and unknown. The jumble of languages: Flemish, French, German, Italian, Greek… the jumble of architecture: medieval, industrial, Art Nouveau, modernist… the jumble of hopes and fears: this was 1984, when the Euro-punks were convinced that President Reagan was a war-mongerer about to bring the world of George Orwell back to life.

This was basically how I spent all my free time for a year, when not swinging a hammer: wandering new streets, trying to catch snippets of conversation, window shopping, discovering the pleasure, normally limited to Belgians and Brits, of sitting at an outdoor café drinking beer in a heavy drizzle. Late night was best, when delivery vans banged more loudly in the otherwise silent streets, and random meetings with Nick Cave's roadies in a back alley after a show jolted us all out of ourselves. I wasn't looking for anything in particular, but I knew the wandering itself was important. I am, and always have been without knowing it, a flaneur.

Questions to Ponder

- How has this place changed over time?
- What sorts of people inhabit this area? How are they similar or different from me?
- How is my life similar to what I see represented in this place?

CHAPTER VII

The City as Meditative Labyrinth

---

*"The city is a labyrinth of streets,
each one leading to a new adventure."—Langston Hughes*

  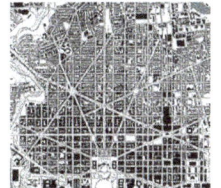

THE GENERAL ASSUMPTION WE HAVE IS THAT CITY streets are not at all a setting for calm spiritual reflection. For that we need to retreat into wild nature; meditation under a waterfall, a mountain top, an oceanside beach will do. Short of that, a quiet room will suffice, with either a minimal look or surrounded by icons, images, and other elements we might gather to assist our focused effort. But as the Zen master Alan Watts reminds us, if you can't meditate in a hot noisy boiler room, you don't know how to meditate. Where else is the need greater for the calm that meditation can bring, after all, than the noisy city street?!

The Story of Labyrinths

Around the world, the walking of meditative labyrinths has become very common. There are organizations dedicated to promoting them, and websites with instructions for designing and building them in one's own back yard. What exactly is this all about?

Most readers will be somewhat familiar with the concept of a labyrinth, at least visually. Typically circular in form, they provide a weaving, back-and-forth pathway for a sort of walking meditation. Leading from outer edge to a defined center and back out again, walking a labyrinth is a meditative process of reflecting on one's life, finding the center, and then reconnecting with the world again, renewed with fresh insight and energy. At times a labyrinth is drawn as a work of art upon which one may meditate.

Historically, labyrinths are often found as a built-in feature of the great medieval cathedrals of Europe. Perhaps the most well-known, fully developed example is embedded in the floor of Chartres Cathedral, in northern France. Further back in history, the ancient Greek world made use of labyrinths. The Celtic world of northern Europe created labyrinths within its landscape. The deepest origin of the very idea of a labyrinth however, might be many thousands of years earlier. Some speculation imagines the source of labyrinths in the Paleolithic cave explorations of tribal shamans. The winding pathways of today's labyrinth symbolically reflect the journeys of those early, specialized spiritual seers and seekers of the unknown as they conducted religious ceremony and spoke with their gods deep inside the earth. Those early cave-dwelling shamans, delving deep into the earth to leave behind for us their amazing artwork, took great physical as well as psychic risks when taking their path. Today our labyrinthine journeys are stripped of any physical danger, but still hold some potential spiritual challenge. The spiritual path is by no means only a source of comfort but may also reveal hidden darkness. Who can say what will be found when seeking to find and confront our soul?

Labyrinth or Maze?

A labyrinth is decidedly not a maze. The experience of a maze is very different from what a labyrinth provides. Mazes are puzzles to be solved, made up of numerous dead ends, false leads, and confusing turns. There is one entrance and a separate exit to be found. Corn mazes have become a great family entertainment. A labyrinth on the other hand, is but one winding path, with no false leads or blind dead ends. After reaching the center, one will retrace the same path to the point of beginning. The path from entrance to center is a process of introspection, discovering elements of one's interior world. The return path, on the same route to the exit, is often a point of reflection on how one is connected to the wider world outside of oneself. So, a maze is an exercise in rational problem solving, while a labyrinth is an effort at intuitive self-exploration.

City Streets as a Template

With all this in mind, I decided to conduct an experiment. As an urban planner, I wondered; could I find a path through city streets which could mimic the winding path of a meditative labyrinth? The selected streets of a city would then become the path of an immersive labyrinth. I was struck that this would likely require making use of multiple methods: the traditional spiritual practice of walking the labyrinth, the more secular observational art of the flaneur, and Thich Naht Hahn's meditative walking.

Yet another meditative practice comes to mind as well. Some readers will no doubt be familiar with the Stations of the Cross. In older Catholic churches, and occasionally in Episcopal and other mainline Protestant denominations, a series of paintings or icons are set around the sanctuary, or embedded in the artwork of stained-glass windows. The images normally depict various episodes in the last week of Christ's life. Church congregants and visitors may meditate upon an image, moving from one to another as a process of private meditation. Traditionally, this was a way for the church to help educate those who could not read, and for those who were unable to make a pilgrimage to Jerusalem.

In the same way that spiritual lessons were artistically embedded into the architecture of a church, so we can develop for ourselves a meditative process of walking through the city streets which we create for ourselves. Think of the pattern of the city – and the world as a whole, for that matter – not as a collection of objects to be manipulated or otherwise dealt with, but as a place where stories are told; your own story.

Dupont Circle: An Example

I chose the Dupont Circle neighborhood of Washington DC as the perfect area to try this out. It lies in the northwest quadrant of the city, above the White House. A number of locations in the neighborhood already carried memory and meaning for me. This area of town has a great variety of excellent streets; grand avenues, leafy residential side streets, quirky alleys. It encompasses part of the downtown office core to the south, transitional mid-town mixed use closer to the Circle itself, and residential areas to the north, both elegant and funky. Having lived in an adjacent neighborhood years ago, and not too far away now, I am quite familiar with this part of the city.

To begin, I developed a template in the form of a 5- layer labyrinth. I chose a square arrangement to accommodate the essentially gridded form of the area. Numerous angled avenues cross the area, which I chose to incorporate as turning points or folded into the otherwise linear arrangement. There are of course innumerable arrangements for labyrinth to take: usually round, but also square, hexagonal, and so forth.

The path I developed along the city streets doesn't precisely mirror the conceptual labyrinth, but close enough. The resulting map I drew to mimic the labyrinth route extends from 14th Street on the east to 24th Street, and from K Street north to T Street. Dupont Circle is thus roughly in the middle of a quite large area of almost 565 acres, an enormous area, almost a mile long on each side. This meant a very long path of almost 8 miles, taking several hours to cover. Certainly, this is more than an ordinary meditative session, and even more than the average flaneur would care to cover. Fortunately, there are more than enough cafes, restaurants, and outdoor park benches for taking a little rest! The typical path of a labyrinth of course includes a process of return. Once a participant reaches the center, they return along the same path for the exit. This mimics the path towards one's center, the soul, and then returning to reconnect with the wider world. Such a return isn't practical for such an already very long path through city streets. We can say then that the experience of such a practice is in and of itself a re-connection to the city. The path itself is at once both an inner experience of the Self, or soul, and an outward journey of connection to the world.

Perhaps one way to phrase my effort is that I am practicing "observational meditation." I am at once taking in my physical surroundings, viewing the activities of my fellow pedestrians and citizens, and my own inner responses to all this. I simply wander, observing, without inner comment or judgement, until perhaps some later time; when I journal at night perhaps. At times it is appropriate to consider my own inner responses to my observations, rather than waiting until another day. Why did I react in that way? What inner conflict of my own did that event on the street corner mimic or reflect? Or I sometimes also question what I see and hear… what is that activity over there all about? And I go to investigate. Or I may merely take note and move on. Not only do I see the same place but the same people. In what ways are they representative of my own various inner personalities? What projections do I throw their way? I may visit at different times of day. The bright sun of high noon, the long shadows of the evening, and late-night streetlamps will each shed different light on the same subject, illuminating distinct values and moods.

At the same time, I attempt to be aware of the small and intimate as well as the grand vista. A little chipmunk skitters under a shrub just as I turn a corner and see that imposing civic building on that distant hill. Small children riding in a carriage behind their parent's bicycle seem to be particularly adept at this way of experiencing the city.

In developing all this, I practiced and explored mostly on my bicycle. In fact, a whole book – two actually – have been written on exactly this approach. The Zen practitioner Juan Carlos Kreimer, a journalist and cycling enthusiast, has developed such a method of "meditative bicycling" in his book, The Bicycle Effect.

Again, this is an extremely large area for a labyrinth, resulting in a very long route so extensive and time consuming that the return route is not practical. So I developed two more smaller secondary routes, also centered on Dupont Circle. A conventional three-layer route, and a small figure-eight path which takes only about 40 minutes. In this way I have a large all-encompassing route that I might follow only once a year; a moderately sized path to follow quarterly or monthly; and a smaller one which I might follow daily or weekly.

Take the time to explore your chosen neighborhood, test out possible routes, create several options on the same or different locations. Perhaps each route might be used for different purposes. Consider the questions below, and develop ones for yourself. And then, go wander.

Questions to Ponder

- Does my community provide an area which I can imagine as a meditative labyrinth?

- What would the center of my "urban labyrinth" be?

- How do the public activities on the streets of my town reflect the inner activities of my psyche?

- Are there significant points or locations in my community which might act in a manner similar to the Stations of the Cross?

CHAPTER VIII

A Process of Introspection

"*If we opened people up, we would find landscapes*"
—*Agnes Varda*

18th and M Streets NW, Washington, D.C.

THE ANCIENT WORDS OF SOCRATES REMAIN TRUE; THE unexamined life is not worth living. It is also valuable to remember that everything one might discover in the examination of the inner world is also to be seen in the outer. As a setting, the city provides an intensification for this process; it is an adventurous setting for your personal mythic Hero's Journey.

Let's bring back the idea found in an earlier chapter, of the process of alchemical reflection. Whether we consider alchemy as process of four steps or seven, certain basic aspects are involved. These include the breaking apart of a whole, examining the parts, transforming those parts, and re-assembling the parts back into a newly formed and integrated whole. For myself, I find the following language to be more easily understood:

- Examine the various aspects of my conscious ego personality;

- Break apart the barrier between my conscious ego and the larger unconscious self;

- Examine and learn to relate to what is found in the unconscious. This involves two stages, a. shadow work or the full acceptance of one's darkest side, and b. develop relationship to and conversation with the anima/ animus (the soul);

- Bring what is found in the unconscious forward, into conscious everyday life – then relate, with body, mind, and soul, and with other individuals in the wider world of shared culture.

Jung described the "spirit of the times," by which he meant the values and assumptions of our shared culture, and the "spirit of the depths" or the life of the soul, as two opposing forces. His task was to bring "the depths" into "the times" and this meant for him as a psychologist to find a way of communicating psychic insight into a culturally acceptable scientific language. For us as lovers of the city, the same task is presented. There is nothing more aligned with "the spirit of the times" than our contemporary urbanism. How do we make a space for the two, the "depths" and the "times" to converse with one another? Our experience of the city is a tool for this, if we bring the right attitude to the task. Let us name it the "useless" city" – emphasize those aspects of the city that are not practical or functional, but "merely" beautiful, inspiring, and poetic. And let us find beauty and meaning in that normally utilitarian infrastructure whose beauty may be hidden.

Consider that the city functions as a mask of God. Just as humans put on a mask – the persona – in order to relate to society, so too must God put on some sort of limiting and acceptable mask in order to interact with humans. This mask is called religion, and is also found in myth and symbol. We can choose to give the city such a role as well, to act as a mask, by which we can personally and collectively relate to the unconscious.

Over time, we as a species are slowly becoming capable of greater understanding of what "god" is. When we think we understand god, this is simply an understanding of some of the "masks" that god wears in order to interact with us. God's persona, if you will. But in becoming familiar with some of those masks, we gain insight into what lies behind.

On Ritual

The places we build today, and even re-build and renovate, rarely have a deep sense of authenticity. Even new development intentionally focused on "place-making" often feel contrived and fake. To a large degree this is due to a lack of history; most development projects seeking to create a "sense of place" are built all at once by large corporate entities. History rarely enters the mix except as a gesture to note its existence.

This lack of a "sense of place" has to do not only with poor design or materials, but a lack of underlying meaning. History of course can supply this; when this too is lacking, meaning can sometimes be created even when not received from the past. Meaning can be infused into a place through ritual. Ritual is of course the re-enactment of a myth or symbol.

We can find examples the use of ritual to infuse memory and meaning into a place in the story of Washington DC, for instance; the foundational ritual of laying the boundary stones, and the corner stones for the Capitol Building, White House, and Washington Monument. Such foundational rituals not only memorialize an event but help create the myth of a place; the foundation of Rome by Romulus when he is purported to have plowed the land around the land that was to become the city is still celebrated, 2,500 years later. This intentionality of creating meaning is crucial today; there are so many places littering our suburban landscapes with no remaining sense of history. A forlorn place may begin to gain meaning, however; a place can be infused with meaning because we choose it to be so. This is our gift to an otherwise unloved place. Such a ritual is one of humility, forgiveness, healing, and hope for a renewed relationship to the land and to history, and as a legacy for the future.

Healing is a central aspect of ritual. There is a distinction between healing and curing. To cure someone is to bring them back to their earlier level of health prior to a wounding or illness. Healing however is much more; it advances the health of the person above and beyond where they were prior to the wounding. With this in mind, we cannot heal the wounds we have inflicted on the earth, only cure them. We do however have the ability to heal the wounds we continue to inflict on our cities and towns, and thus our civilization.

Various ancient rituals of place continue today. One very ancient ritual in the world of placemaking remains the world of construction. Known as "topping out," this ritual is the practice of placing of a tree on the highest point of a building when its construction neared completion. There are numerous histories regarding the source of this practice, some going back to ancient Egypt, when a tree was placed atop a pyramid to honor the deaths of construction workers. Such a ceremony was typically intended to appease the gods or spirits of a place, after disturbing their land. This practice continues today; fir trees can be spotted atop skyscrapers. Another ancient construction ritual can be found in China. Prior to laying the foundation of a house, a priest and feng shui practitioner would be called in to provide ritual protection to the new home. This involved driving a long iron spike into the ground, symbolically nailing the demons of chaos below, preventing them from rising up out of the underworld. A more ordinary ritual for the beginning of a construction project is the ceremonial groundbreaking celebration, in which various project and community leaders gather to turn the first soil, marking the beginning of work with ritual shovels. Such practices serve to advertise and create interest and excitement for the project, but to offer thanks to those who made it possible and those who will undertake the construction itself. Both the beginning and end of construction are times for the expression of gratitude and remembrance. The medieval city was understood by its inhabitants via the role of ritual and procession in civic life. Both local and Christian liturgical celebrations often involved parades and processions, whose routes would include stops at various locations of special significance for ritualized celebration and remembrance.

The rituals above are public and participatory, but for our purposes we must create our own. It is crucial to remember that insights gained from myth, dream, and other processes of inner development, be turned into ritual and moral action. Such rituals, which bring together inner self-development with a place of meaning, can take any number of forms. Like any ritual however, it must become part of a routine, grounded in a particular time and place. The ritual you might create for yourself might take place daily, monthly, or seasonally. It might mean taking a particular route from home to one's place of reflection and meditation, perhaps not the most direct or even attractive, but one associated with placed-based meaning. A personal ritual might involve some object or token, memorable of s specific place, which is carried throughout the day or reserved for some small ceremony in a particular location. Or, such a fetish or totem item might be shared; an example I have seen involves leaving stones with inspirational messages in public but discreet places. A ritual might become elaborated and involve multiple steps, almost ceremonial in structure, such as reciting specific lines of poetry, the placing of some small token or object when sitting at a favored table in a special park, a moment of reflective listening to the surrounding sounds of the city, a remembrance of a person or event associated with the chosen place, drinking a toast of gratitude to the founder of your city, or of acknowledgement to the residents of your own inner city. All of this might be folded into an everyday routine; some options for such everyday actions are described below.

The Everyday

We have discussed in the preceding chapters, the activities of alchemy, flaneury, and meditative labyrinths, as tools of self-reflection in our "psychic classroom" of the city. These might seem rather exotic or at least unexpected undertakings to the general public. There are a number of other more commonplace approaches which can be adapted to one's efforts at self-development through urban experience. These are not always thought of as a spiritual activity, but are generally simple and commonplace efforts. They are normally done without any effort at seeking meaning; my sense has always been that meaning, or insight, will appear of its own accord, perhaps not until long after the activity has ended. I'll run through a few possibilities here.

- **Adopt a Place:** Is there a place that holds significance for you, intrigues you in some fashion? This might be a small park, a particular street corner, some little overlooked nook, or some other public place. Spend time in it and observe how it is used by others. Care for it and relate to it as you might to another person. Perform small acts of kindness for the place; pick up trash, weed the flower beds, or plant some if there are none; report anything broken or in need of repair, such as sidewalk pavement, bench, or fountain. Three examples I have seen can offer inspiration. An informal citizens group in Arlington Virginia has taken on the task of planting and caring for the landscaping within a series of small neighborhood traffic circles which front their homes, relieving the county of such maintenance. A private individual in Washington

DC has also taken on the care and maintenance of a very small triangular park in downtown Washington DC, creating a memorial park honoring a dear friend, available to the public for relaxation. Also in Washington DC, a group of residents has informally gathered together to care for a particular street intersection, keeping it litter-free, watering the street trees and scattering wildflower seeds in place of unkempt weeds.

- **Learn the History:** Who built the town or neighborhood you live in, and when? What is the underlying hydrology and geology? How has the culture changed through the years; was the place used for other purposes? Who were the native peoples who lived and loved this land before the town was built? All these concerns can have an impact on the life you live today.

- **Painting, Drawing, and Photography:** Find a favorite place and interpret it for yourself visually, with your own artistic effort. Capture the mood of the place, and the emotions it evokes in you. This is a very intensely focused way of getting to know a place in detail, with greater depth of meaning. If there isn't a local art school which can provide lessons for the beginner, an excellent online resource can be found at UrbanSketchCourse.com.

- **Writing:** Like the creation of art through painting or sketching, journaling and writing poetry can help us connect to place. This need not be complex; the art of haiku keeps poetry intentionally brief yet allows us to capture depth of feeling. What are the stories and history of the place, what is your experience? Share it publicly, hopefully in the space itself.

- **Buy Local:** Farm markets are a standard first step for this. Quite often there are local crafts people as well as food offerings in such settings. Forego large corporate chains for shopping as often as possible. Although often more expensive, shopping at locally owned businesses strengthens the local community and builds stronger ties with neighbors.

- **Go Car-free:** This might be difficult for most of us. We find ourselves living in a culture that has been completely designed for automobile use for the past 100 years. Basic activities of daily life can be impossible without a car in most places in America. With that in mind, start small. If one day a week proves too difficult, dedicate one a day a month to start. Are there any rare or occasional errands that can be done on foot or bike? If this sort of thing can become a routine, the quality of one's life can improve significantly. The ability to connect with your surroundings directly, rather than through the windshield of a car, gives a more intimate understanding of place.

- **Attend Meetings:** This can be exhausting of course, but it is a fundamental act of caring for and being involved with one's community. Council and planning commission meetings are open to the public and an excellent way of informing oneself and participating in democracy. Other smaller or less known organizational meetings need citizen input as well; does the community have a street tree commission or architectural review board? Neighborhood improvement committees are always in need of volunteers. Attendance and input are improved of course when citizens educate and inform themselves regarding the public good prior to getting involved. Basic public involvement in democracy this level can be considered an act of spiritual healing.

- **Advocate:** Beyond the idea of simply attending public meetings, attend those meetings with the intention of advocating for change. Some ideas are suggested below for communities; advocate for and promote these or others to your community leaders, for the adoption of policies and regulations. Educate yourself and become an invaluable expert.

- **Become a Developer:** This sounds overwhelming and time-consuming, seemingly completely disconnected from spiritual quest; but without a doubt your community is in need of more thoughtful and visionary small-scale property developers. In one sense, every homeowner is a developer. Is there an abandoned building nearby that has become an eyesore, some vacant weed-filled parking lot? Someone should do something about that, and that someone may very well be you. Resources are available for training and support, particularly the Incremental Development Alliance.

Our spiritual task is to come to ever- greater consciousness in order to manage the tension of opposites. I consider this to require not only the tension of psychic opposites but also to increase the awareness of one's physical surroundings; that is, "situational awareness." Where am I? What is occurring around me at this moment? Which way is north? Is there a hint of rain in the air? Are there people nearby who could use my help, even if by simply getting out of their way? Is there some emotional tension in the group of people passing by on the sidewalk? Our lives not only adapt to our environment but also shape it. Our psychic evolution, our spiritual development, is thus a two-way street. We are not swayed by information so much as by stories; we are storytellers at our core. We all tell stories in our own way. If we keep this in mind, all the suggestions above will flow and become manifest more readily.

Dreams

In the highly nebulous field of dream interpretation, it is generally acknowledged that an image of a house symbolizes the interior life of the dreamer. Various rooms might represent aspects of personality or character, for instance. Jung had such a dream, of a house of multiple levels each representing a different stage of history. My dreams too often are dominated by the setting of a house, either mine or that of a person who appears in the dream.

A second dream of Jung's included not merely a house but an entire city. What is referred to as his "Liverpool" dream shaped his understanding of both his personal and professional situation at the time (1927); it redirected his efforts in both as a result. In the dream, he found himself in the city of Liverpool, traveling with several other Swiss. The city was quite dirty and sooty but arranged radially with all the streets converging on a small island at the center. On that central island were found a tree and bright streetlamp. Light and life at the center of an otherwise dismal city. He knew upon reflection that this image represented his own life, and what lay at the center of it. It marked a transition point in both his life and professional research.

Dreams are perhaps the most basic way our unconscious seeks to communicate with us. The general rule is that a dream is trying to tell us something we do not consciously know, and to balance out conscious life. Pay attention to place whenever it appears in a dream. What is the setting in which a dream narrative takes place. Does it hold any meaningful significance? My dreams often include some urban setting as a prominent feature or character; a city as a whole or a small town, a particular street vista, a significant neighborhood from my memory.

The Jungian psychoanalyst Robert Johnson, in his small book *Inner Work*, describes four stages of work with dreams. These are very helpful in making sense of dreams, which can so often seem random and nonsensical. The first stage involves making associations, that is, finding the personal meaning behind the various images that dreams may use. A second step involves making connections between dream images and one's inner dynamic; that is, finding the particular life situations, emotions, and events which the dream is referring to. The third is to make interpretations. What is the dream trying to say, what advice is being given? This should be a natural connection coming out of the first two steps. You should be able to make a simple direct statement to communicate the one main idea of the dream. Such an interpretation is quite personal, so don't rely on any book of dream interpretation. While the interpretation should come as a natural consequence of the first two steps, there may be some false leads at first, and choices to consider. There may be small clues that were overlooked. Keep at it until an aha! moment comes, which might take months or even years. A dream is trying to tell you something you didn't already know. Finally, a dream needs to be made concrete. This might be some small ritual or ceremony, any action really, perhaps not even related to the dream itself in any particular way. It seems that the unconscious wants some sort of recognition that we are paying attention; a dream is not intended to be a one-way event but a two-way conversation. Remember that what is going on here is *relationship*. If we don't seek out the unconscious, then it will seek us out, banging on the door and rapping on the window. Like someone in need demanding attention, it will wreak havoc until it gets the attention and connection it needs and wants.

Active Imagination: The Importance of Non-Existent Places

Delving into the practice of active imagination is significant, filled with both great possibilities and dangers. It involves the most direct relationship with one's unconscious which, it must be remembered, is vastly more powerful and expansive than one's conscious ego, and therefore not to be played with. The unconscious must be approached with care and respect. This is not a practice for everyone; such a relationship can occasionally devolve into psychosis if one becomes overwhelmed by the experience and loses control. It is therefore recommended that someone familiar with the process be available for support. Jungian analysis with an experienced practitioner can provide this.

With that said, its benefits are enormous for those able to make use of it. A definition is in order. Active Imagination is essentially an intentional, interactive waking dream. One does not merely passively observe the images and characters which appear in such a state, as in a dream, but engages and interacts with them, in the moment. It is highly participatory. Here, you have the opportunity to ask questions of your soul, and expect answers. In turn, you will have to provide truthful answers to hard questions posed to you as well. Much of what is revealed will turn out to be startlingly different from opinions and attitudes one consciously holds. The ensuing process generally involves coming to some sort of middle ground, a reconciliation of such opposing stances.

In early attempts at an experience of active imagination, one might feel rather foolish, that it is simply a fake, made-up attempt at creating a fantasy, or nothing more than day-dreaming. And this may be true; but eventually, when one sincerely calls out to the soul, it will answer in one fashion or another. This is a startling and even frightening experience at first. It is crucial that one write down the events, dialogue, and experiences after a session; this helps prevent one from just such a situation of passive day-dreaming.

In the section above, on dreams, a four-step process was outlined as described in Johnson's *Inner Work*. The book also provides a four-step process for active imagination. The first of these is a simple invitation. In an appropriate location which permits a letting go of the outer world, one might simply calmly and quietly ask for those inner characters to appear and begin a conversation. Imagine yourself in a particular place of meaning, make the call, and see who or what appears. A second step involves dialogue. Accept that what is happening is real, that these characters or beings truly have a life of their own, ask them questions and get to know them. They may be shy or gregarious, friendly or intimidating, but they are part of you. The third step involves discovering the various conflicting values and morals that reside within us, as displayed by the characters and situations experienced, and determine how to resolve and integrate it all in a conscious way of life. The characters encountered represent various archetypes, and may seek to dominate and even take over one's life. One must learn to stand up to them, not be overwhelmed by their force, and make moral decisions regarding the advice they give. The final step is equivalent to that for dream work; that is to bring what is found and learned back into everyday life. A process of incarnation, as Johnson puts it. This is not an opportunity to act out the fantasy but to integrate the lesson, either in a ritual form or some practical life habit. This is the importance of the conscious ego, which brings judgement and ethical values into the process.

Having stumbled across the story of Jung's Liverpool dream, described above, a few years ago, I determined to make use of my own fantasy story of a city, in an intentional manner. Since childhood I have carried with me a fantasy world, a small town which I named Harton. It is a relatively small leafy suburb of a larger city which has gone by various names over the years. Much like a novelist might do in creating a setting for a story, I populated my Harton with imaginary friends and favorite locations. Harton has a history and a map, as does the larger city just up the trolley line. I put my youthful world of Harton aside decades ago, but the idea revived itself after reading of Jung's dream.

In my practice of shamanism, I often make use of what is known as "journeying," which is quite similar if not equivalent to Jung's method of active imagination. Both are essentially approaches to interacting with the "other world," whether that be understood as the spirit world of a shaman or the personal unconscious as Jung described it. The methods might appear similar to a meditative state but are anything but calm or relaxing. On the contrary, journeying and active imagination are quite participatory, with the intention of interacting with the various characters one might meet, not merely observing what occurs as in a dream. In this way, Jung sought to externalize various character traits or aspects of personality, personify them, name them, and interact with them, so as to learn from and even manage them when necessary.

I determined to develop my own method of "journeying," for private self-discovery and development. Normally one doesn't choose the manner in which the unconscious presents itself, but I suggested to it a "meeting place." Having posed the question to my unconscious as to whether this was a useful approach, it was accepted and what has developed is essentially the design and exploration of a more intentional vision of Harton, or rather its larger adjacent city. My unconscious decided to make use of this idea and has gone beyond what I expected. The place has morphed as a city into a collection of islands in a lake, divided by natural creeks and formal canals, each a neighborhood unto itself with its own mood and feel. It includes all the elements one expects of a thriving city; stadiums and theaters, industrial works, hotels for temporary visitors, more than one fairly squalid district, a university, hospital, markets, musty old bookstores, a hall of records, on and on. At its heart lies a ceremonial tower which is only accessed by way of a deep watery grotto.

I am now a flaneur of my own imaginary city, my own inner world, my own soul, wandering the streets populated with archetypal characters of my own unconscious Self. I have no hope of getting to know the entire population, and am surprised by the range of citizens who inhabit it, or rather, who inhabit me. There are ordinary and conventional men and women, as well strange characters including a witchy old crone and her protege, a young goddess; mermaids and mermen living in the canals, dwarf-like craftsmen and workers, a magical boat on which I travel, a shadowy thug and an even darker secretive enemy. Every visit includes some small lesson at least, sometimes a shocking adventure and revelation.

These visits most often take place while I sit under my special tree, a Linden or Basswood, along the Potomac River just south of Alexandria. I may meditate prior to beginning, to settle myself into the right frame of openness; but the visits themselves are not meditative or calming at all. While meditation is intended to empty and calm oneself, these journeys are intended to be active, filling and nourishing, like a multi-course meal with friends. My inner journeys begin and end in the same manner and place, on one particular small island to the side of the city, with a particular group of nonhuman companions, my "welcoming committee." The city is at this point far from fully built; early journeys were to a series of dense woods and wetlands with no development at all, a primeval place with only one ancient inhabitant. A series of small villages emerged and have gradually grown together to form a metropolis. It is always under redevelopment, as is any city… or soul.

The highest task of personal development, the most difficult and painful as well as rewarding, is what Jung defined as "individuation," that is, to become what one truly is. Aniela Jaffe, one of Jung's closest associates, describes individuation as the process of making "what fate intends to do with us entirely our own intention." In my own words, it is the process of bringing my conscious intentions for my life into alignment with what my higher Self has planned for me. My conscious ego, the creature which I define as "me," is not truly the author of my life; I am rather an actor on stage, riffing or ad-libbing off a script that I can only partially see. I need to coordinate my role in this play of life with the director, stage manager, and script writer; my soul, my higher Self. This check-in is part of what I do on my journeys.

This has become a regular, intimate way to discover the complexity that lies within me, my relations, and the world around me. What is shared with me by the various characters and situations might be direct and blunt words of advice, or subtle and rather oblique insights, usually confusing and occasionally horrifying. We typically think of the spiritual path as a lonely place to be. What I have found is that my inner life is by no means lonely; I am filled with innumerable invisible characters with whom I may interact. While psychic and spiritual work is private, is by no means isolated. I am not one being, but a multitude.

Three Tasks of Life

The angel Damiel, the central character in the wonderful 1987 movie Wings of Desire, gives us a sense of the enormous gift of incarnation. Bored from his angelic duty of merely witnessing the lives of the humans around him while roaming the streets of post-war Berlin, he becomes despondent because he cannot participate. He tires of knowing everything yet doing nothing. He aches to not know, but to wonder and then discover; to feel pain and taste blood, to experience the emotions of love and joy, loss, and fear. He asks for and is granted the gift of becoming mortal, and his adventures begin.

Like Damiel, we function in this world as temporarily embodied spirits. This incarnation into physicality is not random or accidental I am convinced, but intentional, with various tasks and lessons we are to take on. What these tasks are must be discovered by each of us. For our part, this is the process of awakening into ever-greater consciousness, an enormous and difficult responsibility. As far as I can tell, our various tasks in this process fall into three general categories:

1. Our own personal private process of psychospiritual growth and development. This is our primary task and responsibility. It takes any number of forms and may not look overtly "spiritual" at all. Not only manifested as prayer and meditation, or even the making of art, is included in this; the care and feeding of others, research into the deep

workings of biochemistry, the simple act of conversation with others, maintaining the work of our ancestors as custodians; on and on go the tasks. Growth occurs wherever we apply ourselves, even though we may not be aware of it. Jung described life as having two parts. The first half of life is normally devoted to developing a healthy ego, so that one can contribute positively to the maintenance of society and the benefit of others. The second half, whenever it appears, is intended to learn how to shed the primacy of the ego in an appropriate manner, so that one can begin to rise beyond the limitations of society.

2. Assisting and supporting others in their project of personal development. This can include so many different elements of daily life; to teach, to heal, to support, to simply witness; to play various personal and archetypal roles for each other. From feeding the homeless to entertaining children to planting a flower garden, volunteering for some community or political role, or smiling to the stranger on the sidewalk, we all contribute to each other in countless unexpected and unnoticed ways. Even those interactions which we find unpleasant – arguments and fights, disagreements, confrontations – have their role to play in supporting the growth of another.

3. Creating and maintaining some level of civil order and social structure. This establishes the ongoing stable foundation and context upon which our personal work takes place and is a highly complex task. The creation of order involves more than keeping the lights on and making sure the trains run on time. It can easily, and regularly does, veer off into oppressive regulation and misguided policy. Social justice and equity are never -ending goals. Their achievement requires constant re-evaluation as circumstance changes and insight develops. The choices and connections that our civilization provides us certainly give us freedom, but is there something more important than freedom? If anything, it is perhaps this; what we choose to do with our freedom. Each freedom assumes a corresponding responsibility.

This balancing act of order and chaos brings us into the unavoidable realm of politics. Participation in democracy then arises as a spiritual act – not in seeking any particular religious or political agenda along the spectrum of left and right, but the informed participation in the process itself, for the care and nurture of each other. A passage earlier in this chapter noted the importance of turning insights gained from myth, dream, and other processes of inner development, into ritual and moral action. After having considered the ways we might create personal rituals, those moral actions must be considered here.

A well-functioning democracy requires an enormous amount of private self-reflection and public participation from its citizens. One cannot merely sit back and enjoy the benefits of the freedoms that democracy can provide; democracy demands informed participation, and fundamentally, that participation requires at its base the intentional effort of self-improvement. Could we therefore say that citizenship is a sort of spiritual undertaking, and democracy with its socially connective tissue, is reflective of a religious undertaking?

While this detour into the realm of politics may seem inappropriate for a book such as this, it must be given at least some minimal attention if a psychologically healthier urbanism is to be considered. After all, what could be more political than a city?! Here is the connecting string that I see: Myth tells the story of humans awakening to both the world around them and their inner life, from unconscious instinct to conscious awareness. Then, religion formalizes those mythic stories into ritual and culturally organized shared belief. Politics then operationalizes the values developed in that belief into civic life and mediates the inevitable conflicts. With that in mind, I offer the following five possible elements of successful future democracies: 1. Wide and deep understanding by its citizens of its methods, structures, and processes; 2. Life-long psychological education of self-reflection, self- knowledge, and self-improvement; 3. Empathy for the Other, those unlike oneself, 4. Willingness to compromise and change; 5. Acceptance of connection to something transcendent and eternal, beyond the authority of the state.

The introduction of religion and politics to one another is not in any way a part of the American tradition, for a long list of valid reasons. Yet some sort of neutral territory of mutual acceptance seems necessary. The author Toni Morrison has described herself not as a spiritual person but as "non-secular." Perhaps we can begin to have a vision of a "non-secular" role for the civic commons.

Urban settings, from country hamlet to megalopolis, support these three tasks in ways the natural world cannot. We find both the setting and the tools in urbanism because we are a fundamentally social species. Spiritual development may be a personal journey but by no means is it an isolated one. We are connected to one another with both visible and invisible ties. We act out of evolved instinct just as other species; but we also act out of intention.

Though a social species, our experience of physical incarnation subjects us to a profound fragmentation which cannot be undone. We will experience wholeness on the other side of the veil, so to speak. Incarnated life is the intentional, or at least unavoidable, experience of limitation and brokenness. All these tasks of humanity are to discover eternal truth by the experience of temporal life. Learning how to repair broken connections is a fundamental and essential lesson of life. Life together in all our urban patterns is the place, and the method we use to work it out.

You Are A City: Urbanism as a Tool for Expanding Spiritual Horizons

We are spirits embodied in the physical realm with the intention of discovering the eternal through our experience of the temporal. This is an evolutionary process of gradual awakening, with various steps or stages involved. As purely instinctual animals deep in our evolutionary past, we acted before we understood why. We then began to create images or symbols which represented those actions. We next began to tell stories about those actions. Only after that did we become aware of the meanings and deeper purposes behind those actions, and only poorly at first. Over the millennia, we began to understand, little by little, what we had experienced. This is the process of coming out of darkness and into the light of conscious awareness. We still, after all these thousands of years, see through a glass very darkly.

We have only very recently begun to recognize the evolution of our species biologically and how that primordial pre-history has acted as a foundation for myth and the narrative of religion. We can now also see the evolution of myth and religion over thousands of years, and how stories build on the past and evolve in their attempt to explain the world and how to act in it. From the early creation stories of the Mesopotamians, to those of the Egyptians, of the Israelites who grew out of their experience during enslavement under those; and then on to the Christian narrative, there is a history of a desire to understand our place in the world. Each of these acted as a foundation and teacher for the next, more integrated mythic story of spiritual development. Each new narrative has not so much displaced the previous but incorporated its wisdom and transcended it by providing a larger vision; usually by transcending boundaries of culture. Carl Jung saw the string extending further back into deepest prehistory, and then forward, to include the Gnostics and eventually the alchemists whom he saw as the culmination of the Christian tradition. Thus, what we can anticipate in future generations is not an end to the Christian tradition so much as its transformation and extension into an ever- larger vision with a wholly new yet familiar myth that echoes all the previous. An update not simply in the content of the story but in the language and metaphor.

With all that in mind, our understanding of what a city can provide must also evolve. We must ask more of a city than we have; or at least to the level of our ancestors. That it provides not merely shelter and efficient commerce and entertainment, but act as the repository of our highest insights, to assist us in the quest to discover those callings and aspirations, both public and private; and to be designed expressly for that purpose. We are filled with information and knowledge, in our unconscious and our souls, of which we are not even aware. Our experience of cities can be of enormous assistance in bringing this imbedded knowledge into the open. Given Jung's understanding of individuation, that our highest calling is the growth and development of our soul, the immersive city of intention can and ought to be an enormous support.

As various mythic traditions tell us, the original sin was to become conscious. This is the Greek story of Prometheus, who stole fire from the gods and gave it to humans; Pandora's Box; the Mesopotamian drama of Tiamat and Apsu; and most familiar to us, that of Adam and Eve in the Garden of Eden. We have been struggling to manage this horrible gift, which none of us would ever choose to do without, ever since. The subsequent sin is now its opposite; to remain not fully and completely conscious, to remain semi-awake, or even to desire to return to the unconscious womb. We shouldn't have become conscious in the first place, many would say; it is a huge burden of responsibility that we have never been able to live up to. Better to have remained in our pure animal nature, acting purely on instinct, without any conscious intentionality. But the creator of consciousness seems to have found it advantageous for us to acquire it. It is our assigned task to become ever more consciously aware as a service to "the gods." Once awakened, being half awake is worse. We remain subject to our animal instinct but with no understanding or control, or worse, to misunderstand and act out of an inaccurate vision. All in or not at all; there is no stopping or turning back. To a large degree, the task seems to be the integration of opposites; that is, how to deal with and accept both darkness as well as light, good and evil, rationality and the mystic. We appropriately seek out religion in that process, to provide comfort and security. But a spiritual path is precisely not secure; it is filled with discomfort and uncertainty. Both have a place in our personal and cultural development. The experience of urbanism provides the setting for each, for in it we discover how to operate not only in the natural world but the human.

For the urbanist a particular responsibility emerges from this. The places we build and imagine reflect the values we hold. If we anticipate a continuing evolutionary growth in our consciousness, our conception of urbanism must develop as well. The places we inhabit must be so much more than technically competent and bureaucratically efficient. These are the places which ought to challenge us to rise to our highest visions. From their earliest inception, cities have acted as the physical embodiment of these visions. But for too long, our rationality and analytical science have taught us to look down, reducing our horizons and vision.

As embodied spirits with the fundamental task of educating ourselves, the physical world is our school. We build cities as repositories of the lessons we have learned. Consider that the zodiac was developed thousands of years ago as a memory aid, a library filing system where stories and information could be kept available. The zodiac is a collection of symbolic stories by which cultural and spiritual values were maintained. As the centuries have marched on, we have collected many more stories, which we can imbed in the physical design of the places we build, as did our ancestors to a greater or lesser extent. One of the enduring tasks of a city is the discovery, creation, storage, and dissemination of our accumulated knowledge.

We are foragers, and have been for pretty much our entire evolutionary history. This we share with other species, to forage for food in order to survive; what distinguishes us is what we forage for. We are foragers not simply for food but for information, which allows us not merely to survive at the moment but to flourish over time by planning for the future. The city, with its vast resources and connections, makes this infinitely more possible, the internet notwithstanding. The city can thus not only contain a library but becomes itself an enormous library and classroom. Walking the streets is akin to browsing all the aisles and bookshelves, filled with cultural and spiritual knowledge. Any space can become sacred, depending on what the visitor carries with them. But space itself can provoke or remind the visitor if designed to do so; if its shelves have been stocked with the correct books, so to speak.

Since western civilization has largely given up on traditional mythology and the Christian story, many westerners look to the eastern traditions, particularly Buddhism, as a substitute. But the essential teachings of Judeo-Christian heritage are too deeply embedded, down into our cultural DNA, to walk away from; nor is there really any need to. The coming age may very well focus on the reconciliation/ assimilation of opposites. Politics goes only so far, not nearly deeply enough, and cannot supply a viable alternative. The biggest limitation to a developing civilization is the psychological makeup of individuals. Religious institutions like the church were, at least partially, attempts to psychologically develop the population on a mass scale toward ever-greater psychic maturity. To the extent such institutions fail, it is not so much that religion is itself the cause of suffering, but that institutions are by their very nature susceptible to being hijacked by the darkest side of our individual natures.

The crisis of the modern world is the lack of life-affirming stories. Or rather, we are surrounded by mythic stories that we no longer know how to use or learn from. Humans need an operating system… our old "MS DOS" of Christianity has done all the work it can for us and has degraded over time by the patches and "upgrades" of narrow-minded cultural assumptions and scientific rationalism. It now needs more than just an upgrade, just as we might replace DOS with Linux. The essential traits and truths of the Christian heritage must be incorporated into something larger.

We live through story and narrative. We understand the world not merely as a set of discreet objects, but in how we relate to those objects; those objects making up the world are characters in a story and so are we. How do we interact with all see and experience in the world? What role does this thing, this place, this person, play in my life, and me in theirs? Can we build such questions into a city physically, into the form and fabric of the urban pattern, intentionally? Our ancestors had that ability, and our task is to understand how they did so and make use of it. We must understand the past in order to gain a sense of who we are today, and what we need to create for the future.

A city built only for the purposes of efficiency, security, commerce entertainment, or even happiness will not reach its potential; though these are crucial aspects, they can easily devolve into mere distraction. Much of what passes for urban "placemaking" today revolves around the "Disneyfication" of downtown; witness Times Square in New York City. The design of a deeper urbanism can provoke us to create meaning and purpose, individually and culturally. Entertainment is a distraction when we have lost a sense of meaning and purpose. As Victor Frankl phrases it, "When a person cannot find a deep sense of meaning, they distract themselves with pleasure." Our culture has reached that point.

The process of psychological growth involves having our self-conceptions and assumptions shattered, so that we can examine the pieces and re-assemble ourselves into a more expansive and intentional Self. We must understand the parts, in other words, in order to approach the Whole. Civilizations throughout history go through that same process. The experience of this shattering and reformation of culture has taken place over the last several hundred years as rationality of science and technology have come to dominate. We can think of science and technology as a process of the destructive shattering our unified spiritual sense of the world, in order to understand the parts. It has been painful and dangerous, even deeply harmful in numerous ways—the ecological damage we have learned to cause is evidence enough of that. Yet in this way too our understanding of reality is expanded. The task collectively is like that of the individual; to weave together the teachings of both spirit and matter, science and soul, into a unified vision. Almost every effort to improve the world begins and ends with a desire to change the thinking, habits, and behaviors of other people. Regard with suspicion any approach at "saving the world" unless it is accompanied by an equal or greater effort to change oneself. Conversely, any approach to change oneself must be accompanied by participation in the world.

Infusing our experience of urban places with meaning is therefore a critical need. When we love and care for a place – just as for a person – we will care for its context and wider setting as well. The natural environment is the context for urbanism. Thus, the love, repair, and healing of urban places is a vital aspect of our care for the earth. In this, the human body is analogous to the city; it is never truly completely "healthy;" there is always some small nick, some infection, some system in need of repair. Urban places too are always going through some process of repair and renovation, and thus are incomplete and in the process of healing. The healing of urbanism requires a renewed infusion of meaning and purpose.

The experience one has of urbanism, whether grand city or small town, is largely dependent upon the inner life one brings along to the moment. In turn though, urban form and its program impacts one's inner world. The two build upon one another. Both benefit when the design of place, and the individual life, are approached with intentionality.

The human brain is the most complex structure in the universe, so far as we know. It represents the highest concentration of consciousness, both intellectual and of spiritual or psychic energy, in the physical universe. A city is the highest concentration of humans, with all their individual and collective aspirations, hopes and weaknesses. What are the implications of this? The strongest motivations we have arise out of the unconscious, which makes up the vast majority of our being. How do we find out what the unconscious wants? Through images seen in dreams, symbols, visions, and recurring patterns in the stories of mythology and religion over thousands of years. When we experience the city as an immersive environment to promote the conversation between ego and soul, we can align ourselves with our larger intentions and manifest these aspirations more fully and on a daily basis. "Formlessness seems to be practically the equivalent of unconsciousness," as Jung reminds us. Understanding the form of our physical environment and discovering meaning there is thus an essential aspect of coming to consciousness.

Apocalyptic Christianity and new age thinking aside, we are without doubt entering a new era. Aquarius, the water-bearer, is slowly emerging. The coming of this water symbol in the zodiac above coincides with sea level rise, both of which threaten to wash away so much of what we have built over the past centuries, both physically and metaphorically. Water traditionally symbolizes the mysterious and dangerous depths of the human soul. These two together, the metaphorical Aquarius and the existential threat of inundation by rising seawater, comprise a call to us for deeper reflection and new direction. In response to this, I see two new and essential roles for urbanism: to intentionally act as the physical structure in support of private, individual spiritual or psychological growth; and to also act as the physical infrastructure supporting a new and as-yet unformed spiritual cosmology which may act as the foundation of some future cultural myth of expanded and more balanced inclusiveness.

Such a perspective on the city is much like the medieval process of alchemy. The intention of such an alchemy is not only the redemption and healing of the individual but the release of god, or spirit, from imprisonment in matter. The transformation of matter – the city – and the transformation of soul are equivalent. In this process we are being used as vessels by psychic forces far larger than we, as tools of conscious experience and growth. We have no choice but to rise to the challenge.

Questions to Ponder

- What elements of my city would I like to discuss with my soul?

- What insights about myself have I gained by observing places around me?

- How do the various parts of my city reflect my own inner landscape?

Afterword

The great lesson from the true mystics is that the sacred is in the ordinary, that it is to be found in one's daily life, in one's neighbors, friends, and family, in one's back yard. —Abraham Maslow

The preceding pages have covered an array of ideas regarding cities, soul, and techniques for exploring each. We have discussed various methods and techniques of self-reflection, such as flaneury, alchemy, the meditative labyrinth, and Jungian individuation, and how the city can play a supporting role in that process. In all this, the built environment becomes the objective place in which we manifest the subjective.

The physical city is an extension of our bodies. The body contains the soul, the city is a container holding a collection of embodied souls… the spaces we inhabit act as an extension of our body. This is true for us all, and so we delve more deeply into our inner life we also become joined together in empathy and understanding; not "at the hip," as the saying goes, but "joined at the city."

Spiritual traditions from every corner of the world are filled with advanced mystical teachers and practitioners who reached higher levels of awareness and insight via "abstention from the dirt." But must this be the only way? A Jungian approach includes working with the darkness, not avoiding it, just as this sort of spiritual familiarity with the dark side is fundamental to the ways of the traditional shaman. The city is as "dirty" as life in this world gets. If there is *any* spiritual intention in our incarnation as evolving containers of soul in this physical world, then our goal cannot be to ignore, avoid, or deny the settings in which we find ourselves. We must therefore learn to experience "dirty" urbanism – not only "pure" nature – as sacred space. As the Zen teacher Alan Watts reminds us, "If you can't meditate in a hot noisy boiler room, you don't know how to meditate."

As I strove to finish this book and bring my thoughts to something approaching a conclusion, I found a nagging question kept appearing in front of me, insisting that I pay attention to it. What is the distinction between spirit and soul?

I tend to use the two interchangeably, as I think many of us do today. Yet in the ancient world, they were distinct from one another, so that each of us had a tripartite nature: body (ego), soul, and spirit. Soul played the role of intermediary between the physically embodied conscious ego and ethereal spirit. Around the 8th Century though a change in understanding apparently occurred within the Christian church, so that soul and spirit were more interchangeable. The tripartite division was reduced to spirit and body.

Perhaps we need to consider a return to the old understanding. Thomas Moore, the spiritual writer, speaks to the roles of each: "In the best situations it isn't easy to distinguish spirit from soul because both play important roles in everything we do. But making the distinction gives the deep soul its due. Spirit inspires, while soul delves deep into the complexities of an issue. Spirit likes to have a planning meeting; soul likes to have a long and deep conversation. Spirit sets goals; soul plods along, going deep all the way. Spirit prefers detachment, while soul sinks into its attachment to places, people, and home. The two dimensions are both important and valuable. You don't need to balance them because balance is too perfect, a spirit idea in the first place. It's enough to give each what it wants and needs in the moment."

Perhaps we can think of spirit being at the mountain peak, soul in the valleys; we speak of spiritual enlightenment which takes us away from the earth towards the heavens, but soulfulness is in the here and now. Giving respect to each is essential. A quote from the teacher Toko-pa Turner summarizes this well: "The focus on enlightenment rather than embodiment distances us from the messy business of being human. If you're doing it right, presence, rather than detaching you, sensitizes you to your environment. It puts you smack-dab in the discomfort, the disagreeability, the pain, the awkwardness, and the contradiction – this is where you grow more skilled at meeting life where it's at, rather than how you'd prefer it to be. In other words, allowing the full spectrum of events to be included in your experience, rather than mounting resistance to them."

We think of spirit as pure, clean, and pristine. But soul will get dirty with you. Soul can be found sitting in a grubby back alley.

Just as we humans have evolved biologically and psychically – and continue to do so – so must our vision of what a city can be. Much of this involves re-learning what the past once knew. The spiritual city is the soulful city. Not away from the pain of the world but through the dirt, is the way of growth. To reach the pure spirit our path will take us through the impure soul. Is the city more a soulful, rather than spiritual, experience?

Humans spent tens of thousands of years in ancient matriarchal structures; we are now in the seemingly final stages of several thousand years of patriarchal systems. What is the next stage of our awakening, of union and balance? Psychically and culturally but also physically, urbanistically; how will we organize ourselves in response to whatever mythology emerges to represent that union? What impact does that have on our built environment and how we experience it? Cities only emerged during and as a result of patriarchal systems, representing the physical embodiment of a patriarchal order of logic and rationality. How must they change in nature to reflect a unity with a more soulful and intuitive matriarchal perspective? To discover this will be a fundamental task of urbanism in the coming times. Perhaps what we are faced with is not so much the reconciliation of opposites, as Jung phrased it, but of respecting and valuing, delighting in, making use of the "complimentaries" found in city and nature. That feels more soulful.

Sources and Further Reading

Below is found a short list of sources used in the development of this work, a series of books that have inspired me in my own journey. I hope these inspire you as well and promote an ongoing curiosity.

- *A Religion of One's Own* by Thomas Moore
- *A Short History of Myth* by Karen Armstrong
- *City and Soul* by James Hillman
- *History and Origins of Consciousness* by Erich Neuman
- *How to Walk* by Thich Naht Han
- *Inner Work* by Robert Johnson
- *Invisible Cities* by Italo Calvino
- *Man and His Symbols* by Carl Jung
- *Memories Dream Reflections* by Carl Jung
- *Myths to Live By* by Joseph Campbell
- *Suburban Nation* by Andres Duany
- *The Sacred Geometry of Washington DC* by Nicholas Mann

www.ingramcontent.com/pod-product-compliance
Lightning Source LLC
Chambersburg PA
CBHW071118160426
43196CB00013B/2611